MUSLIM
RELIGIOUS ARCHITECTURE

INSTITUTE OF RELIGIOUS ICONOGRAPHY
STATE UNIVERSITY GRONINGEN

ICONOGRAPHY OF RELIGIONS

EDITED BY

TH. P. VAN BAAREN, L. LEERTOUWER, F. LEEMHUIS and H. BUNING (*Secretary*)

SECTION XXII: ISLAM

FASCICLE TWO

LEIDEN
E. J. BRILL
1974

MUSLIM RELIGIOUS ARCHITECTURE

PART I

THE MOSQUE AND ITS EARLY DEVELOPMENT

BY

DOĞAN KUBAN
Professor of History of Architecture
Istanbul Technical University

With 9 figures and 44 plates

LEIDEN
E. J. BRILL
1974

ISBN 90 04 03813 2

PRINTED IN THE NETHERLANDS

CONTENTS

ACKNOWLEDGEMENTS

My gratitude goes to all those scholars in the field of Islamic Art and Archaeology whose works made a limited introduction such as this to Islamic Religious Architecture possible.

The sources for the plans and the photographs are indicated on p. 25 ff.

SELECT BIBLIOGRAPHY

Abbreviations in the text:

EI Encyclopedia of Islam, English edition.
EMA Creswell, Early Muslim Architecture.
MAE Creswell, Muslim Architecture in Egypt.

AHMAD FIKRY, *L'art islamique en Tunisie. La grande mosquée de Kairouan,* Paris, 1936.

BECKER, C. H., "Die Kanzel im Kultus des alten Islams", *Orientalische Studien (Theodor Nöldeke Festschrift),* Giessen, 1906, pp. 331-51.

BOUSQUET, G. H., *Les grandes pratiques rituelles de l'Islam,* Paris, 1949.

BUKHARI, Y. K., "The mosque architecture of the Mughals", *Indo-Iranica,* IX/2 (1956), pp. 35-42.

BURTON, R. F., *Personal narrative of a pilgrimage to el-Medinah and Meccah,* London, 1855-56, 3 vols.

CHAGATAI, M. A., "Mosques in the Indo-Pakistan Sub-continent during the first century of Islam, and their architecture", *Iqbal,* X/3 (1962), pp. 42-54.

CRESWELL, K. A. C., "The evolution of the minaret, with special reference to Egypt", *Burlington Magazine,* XLVIII (1926), pp. 134-140, 252-258, 290-298.

——, *Early Muslim architecture,* Oxford, 1932-1940, 2 vols.

——, *A short account of early Muslim architecture,* Pelican, Harmondsworth, 1958.

——, *A bibliography of the architecture, arts, and crafts in Islam,* London, 1961.

——, art. "Architecture", *EI*², 1960.

DIEZ, E., *Die Kunst der islamischen Völker,* Berlin, 1915.

——, *Churasanische Baudenkmaeler,* Berlin, 1918.

——, *Persien, islamische Baukunst in Churasan,* Hagen, 1923.

——, Art. "Manāra", *EI*¹, III (1929), pp. 227-31.

——, Art. "Miḥrāb", *EI*¹, III (1931), pp. 485-90.

——, Art. "Minbar", *EI*¹, III (1936).

——, Art. "Qubba", *EI*¹, *Supplement* (1937), pp. 127-34.

ERDMANN, K., "Die Sonderstellung der anatolischen Moschee des XII. Jahrhunderts", *First International Congress of Turkish Arts, Ankara, 1959, Communications,* 1961, pp. 94-101.

GODARD, A., "Le Tari-Khana de Damghan", *Gazette des beaux-arts,* XII (1934), pp. 225-35.

——, "Historique de la Masdjid-é Djum'a d'Isfahān", *Athar-é Iran,* I (1936), pp. 213-82.

——, "L'origine de la madrasa, de la mosquée et du caravan-sérail à quatre iwans", *Ars Islamica,* XV-XVI (1951), pp. 1-9.

——, "Les anciennes mosquées de l'Iran", *Arts asiatiques,* III (1956), pp. 48-63, 83-88.

——, *L'art de l'Iran,* Paris, 1962.

GOLOMBEK, L., "Abbasid Mosque at Balkh", *Oriental art,* XV/3 (1969) pp. 1-17.

GRABAR, O., "La grande mosquée de Damas et les origines architecturales de la mosquée", *Synthronon, Art et Archéologie de la fin de l'Antiquité et du Moyen Âge, Recueil d'Études,* 1968, pp. 107-114.

——, "The architecture of the Middle Eastern city from past to present: The case of the mosque", in I. M. Lapidus (ed.), *Middle Eastern cities, A symposium,* Berkeley and Los Angeles, 1969, pp. 26-46.

HAUTECOEUR, L. Y et G. WIET, *Les mosquées du Caire,* Paris, 1932, 2 vols.

HAMILTON, R. W., *The structural history of the Aqsā Mosque,* Jerusalem, 1940.

HAMMAD, M., "L'évolution de la chaire dans la vie religieuse en Egypte", *Cahier historique égyptien,* 8 (1956), pp. 117-29.

HERZFELD, E., *Geschichte der Stadt Samarra,* Hamburg, 1948.

HÖVER, O., *Kultbauten des Islams,* Leipzig, 1922.

JIMENEZ, F. H., "El almimbar movil del siglo X de la mezquita de Cordoba", *al-Andalus,* 24 (1959), pp. 381-99.

KUBAN, D., *Anadolu-Türk mimarisinin kaynak ve sorunları,* Istanbul, 1965.

KÜHNEL, E., *Die Moschee: Bedeutung, Einrichtung und kunsthistorische Entwicklung der islamischen Kultstätte,* Berlin, 1949.

LAMBERT, E., "Les origines de la mosquée et l'architecture religieuse des Omeyyades", *Studia Islamica*, VI (1956), pp. 5-18.
LÉZINE-SEBAG, P., "Remarques sur l'histoire de la Grande Mosquée de Kairouan", *Revue de l'Institut des Belles-Lettres Arabes à Tunis*, 25 (1962-63), pp. 245-256.
MAHMUD AKKUSH, "Contribution à une étude des origines de architecture musulmane: La Grande Mosqué de Médine (al-ḥaram al-Madanī), *Mélanges Maspero*, III (1940), pp. 377-410.
MARÇAIS, G., "L'église et la mosquée", *L'Islam et l'Occident*, Marseille, 1947, pp. 174-184.
——, *L' architecture musulmane d'Occident*, Paris, 1954
MIELCK, R., "Zur Geschichte der Kanzel im Islam", *Der Islam*, XIII/1-2 (1923), pp. 109-112.
MILES, G. C., "Miḥrāb and Anazah: A study in Early Islamic iconography" *Archaeologia Orientalia in Memoriam Ernst Herzfeld*, Augustin, Locust Valley, 1952, pp. 156-71.
MONNERET DE VILLARD, U., *Introduzione allo Studio dell'archaeologia Islamica*, Venezia-Roma, 1966.
Moslem Religious Board of Central Asia and Kazakhstan, *Historical Monuments of Islam in the U.S.S.R.*, Tashkent, undated.
PEDERSEN, J., E. DIEZ, R. A. KERN, art. "Masdjid", *EI*¹, III (1930), pp. 314-89.
PIJOAN, J., *Arte Islamico*, Madrid, 1949.
POPE, A. U. and others, *A survey of Persian art*, Oxford, vols. II, and IV.
PUGACHENKOVA, G. A., *Puti Razvitia arkhitektury iuzhnogo Turkmenistana*, Moscow, 1958.
RIVOIRA, G. T., *Architettura musulmana, sue origini e suo sviluppo*, Milano, 1914.
SALADIN, H., *La mosquée de Sidi Okba à Kairouan*, Paris, 1923.
SARRE, F., and E. HERZFELD, *Archaeologische Reise im Euphrat- und Tigris-Gebiet*, Berlin, 1912-20.
SAUVAGET, J., "Observations sur quelques mosquées Seldjoukides", *Annales de l'Institut d'Études Orientales*, Tome IV (1938), pp. 81-120.
——, *La mosquée omeyyade de Médine*, Paris, 1947.
SERGEANT, R. B., "Miḥrāb", *Bulletin of the School of Oriental and African Studies*, 22 (1959), pp. 439-53.
SNOUCK HURGRONJE, C., *Mekka*, Leyden, 1931, 2 vols.
STERN, H., "Les origines de l'architecture de la mosquée omeyyade", *Syria*, vol. XXVIII (1951), pp. 269-79.
THIERSCH, H., *Pharos, Antike, Islam und Okzident: ein Beitrag zur Architekturgeschichte*, Leipzig und Berlin, 1909.
TORRES BALBAS, L., *La mezquita de Cordoba y las ruinas de Madinat al-Zahra*, Los Monumentos Cardinales de España, vol. XIII, Madrid, 1952.
——, "Origen de las disposiciones arquitectonicas de las mezquitas", *Al-Andalus*, XVII (1952), pp. 388-99.
WENSINCK, A. J., art. "Kaᶜba", *EI*¹, II (1924), pp. 584-92.
——, art. "Muṣallā", *EI*¹, III, (1936), pp. 805-6.
WIET, G. and others, *Répertoire chronologique d'épigraphie arabe*, Cairo, 1931ff.
WÜSTENFELD, F., *Geschichte der Stadt Mekka, nach den arabischen Chroniken bearbeitet*, Leipzig, 1861.
ZWEMER, S. M., "The pulpit in Islam", *The Moslem World*, XXIII (1933), pp. 217-29.

FOREWORD

In this brief outline only those aspects of Muslim architecture which are directly related to the religious content of Muslim culture are described. The functional character of the formal development was our main concern. Thus the first fascicle is an introduction to the mosque and its early history. The second fascicle will deal with the development of religious buildings in later periods and will include general definitions of the later building types: the tomb, the madrasa and the convent.

The house of the Prophet, which by the time of ʿUmar became a proper *masjid,* seems to have contained all the essential elements of the Muslim house of worship. For all later developments, it was a basic reference, and we might say that the first mosque had the vigor of *sunna*. The tomb, *madrasa* and convent were later creations within the atmosphere of non-Arab Muslim cultures. Although early Islam categorically took a strong stand against tomb buildings, *madrasas* and convents found their place in orthodox Muslim culture with reasonable ease. And functionally, they formed a rather organic relationship with the early mosque tradition.

It will appear obvious if one looks to the architectural realizations of the Muslim countries from a religious viewpoint that the content remains solidy homogeneous throughout the ages.

D. KUBAN

I

THE MOSQUE [1]

Consonant with the character of Islam, which welds together the secular and the sacred and expresses them by means of a unified and rigid behaviorial doctrine, its house of worship has been the center of social life for all Muslim communities throughout their history. Hence, in addition to its main function as a place for prayer, within its precincts the mosque has provided space for social functions such as education, community gatherings, shelter for travellers and food distribution to the poor. In later periods of Islamic history there developed specific building forms for these various functions once associated with the central one of prayer, culminating with the foundation of great religious complexes by the Mamlūks, the Tīmurīds and the Ottomans. Nevertheless, the evolution of the formal aspects of the mosque design was most directly influenced by considerations of its primary function, namely as a space for prayer in common.

The daily life of a true believer is interwoven with his foremost ceremonial duty, the *ṣalāh*. Although the time and frequency originally set forth are not known with certainty, the ritual elements of *ṣalāh* were already determined during the Prophet's lifetime or, at the latest, during the rule of the Umayyads, and is prescribed by the Koran. Before we outline the fully developed Muslim ritual and its cult objects and requirements in space organization, however, it is necessary to observe the growth of the Muslim house of worship during the lifetime of the Prophet.

The First Mosque

Before the Hijra, Muslims had no special place for prayer in Mecca and the followers of Mohammed gathered in private. The Prophet himself is related to have had his prayers occasionally near the Kaʿba. Any temple built in previous periods could fulfill the function of a prayer place, *masjid*,[2] since there was no other god but Allāh; nor did Muslims seek a covered space for the *ṣalāh* for, as an *ḥadīth* says, "All the world is a *masjid*." [3]

After Mohammed arrived in Medina, a simple house of mud brick on a stone foundation was built for him and his family. Opening onto the courtyard there was, to the north, a shelter, *Ẓulla*, built with palmtree trunks which supported a roof of palm leaves and mud. And "one could touch the roof with one's hand." [4] The *Ẓulla*, used as the place for prayer, faced the direction of Jerusalem, but when, later, *ṣalāh* was executed facing Mecca,[5]

---

[1] See for a full account: Pedersen, article 'Masdjid', in *EI*[1], vol. III, pp. 315-376; Cresswell, *EMA* I, pp. 1.

[2] The word *masjid* is used in the Koran to express pre-Islamic temples and even mausoleums: Pedersen, *op. cit.*, p. 315.

[3] According to Ibn Hishām quoted by Pedersen, *op. cit.*, p. 316.

[4] Ibn Saʿd, quoted by Creswell, *A short account of early Muslim architecture*, Pelican, 1958, p. 3.

[5] Koran II: 141 explains the reason for this change. The *masjid* in which this occurred, probably the *muṣallā* of the Banu Salima outside Medina, was called *al-Masjid al-Qiblatain*.

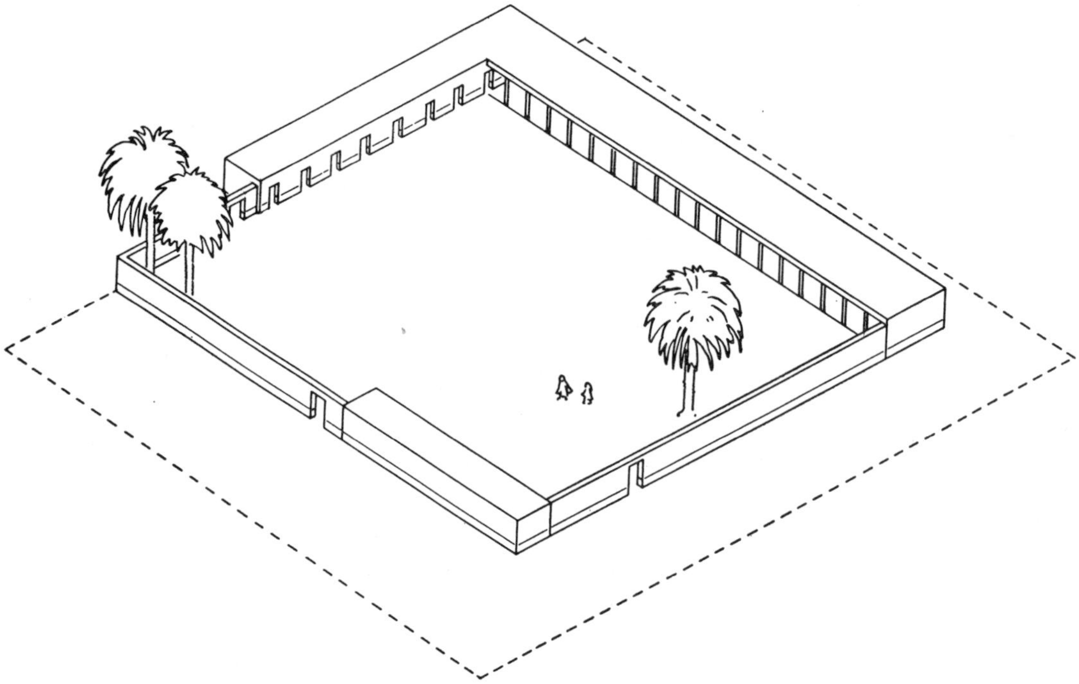

Fig. 1. The house of the Prophet—Reconstruction.

another portico was built on the south side. On the east side of the courtyard small rooms, *ḥujra*, were built for the Prophet's wives, each opening onto the courtyard. (In A.D. 707 when they were demolished there were, in all, nine such apartments.) And finally, in one corner of the courtyard, opposite the *Ẓulla*, there was a smaller shelter, *Ṣuffa*, for the visitors or poor to stay overnight.[1] (Fig. 1).

In Medina, other places for worship were available. On the estates of Salima, for instance, in an open prayer place which is called *al-Muṣallā*[2] special public prayers, such as those for important feast days, *ṣalāt al-ʿīd*, were held. In these open places of worship a small wall or an object, *ṣutra*, was used to indicate the direction of Mecca. All prayer places, open or covered, served other functions as well, as for example, executions took place in the *muṣallā*s; and the Prophet's own house was the seat of the government. But with the passing of time the requirements of religious ritual were met and determined the basic form of the mosque which has remained throughout Muslim history, essentially unaltered.

The Ritual of *Ṣalāh* and Functional Elements in a Mosque Associated with it

For the prayer in common the believers gather in a mosque. The Muslim prayer, *ṣalāh*, is a well defined ritual. It has to be performed in parallel rows, in order to follow the movements of a leader, *imām*, and to face Mecca. The direction of Mecca is called the *qibla*. The act of *ṣalāh* culminates in prosternation, *sujūd*, from which comes the word

---

[1] This can be considered the origin of the later hospice buildings connected with the mosques.
[2] A. J. Wensinck, article '*Muṣallā*', in *EI*[1], vol. III, p. 746.

masjid, the place to prostrate before God. Physically the constitution of rows indicates the main spatial direction to which a prayer hall should correspond. The early mosque plan was a clear and simple answer to this exigency.

In the course of time other basic requirements connected with *ṣalāh* gave birth to the essential elements of a mosque: the believers must be called together at the appointed times; a structure had to be provided from which the call, (*adhān*), could be heard by all; a high platform or tower, a minaret provides for this necessity. Bodily purification is necessary before the prayer, thus a basin or fountain was conveniently placed outside the prayer hall for ablution, *wuḍū'* or *ghusl.* For the leader of the congregation, the *imām,* a defined place was necessary, which led to the insertion of a niche, *miḥrāb,* into the wall which faced Mecca. A sermon, *khuṭba,* has to be delivered, thus a pulpit, *minbar,* which consists of a stairway leading to a small platform was devised. And probably from the time of the first Umayyad caliph, Muʿāwiya, a secluded space, *maqṣūra,* was required for the caliphs or governors who were not only the political leaders but who also fulfilled the functions of the *imām* on Fridays.

Although the Muslim prayer may be performed anywhere, traditionally, prayer in common has been held in higher esteem and is obligatory for the Friday noon service, *ṣalāt al-jumʿa,* which is usually accompanied by a *khuṭba.* However, for some religious reformers, especially al-Shāfiʿī, a Friday noon prayer required at least forty believers to be present. Therefore only certain mosques were allowed to have a *minbar,* which became the symbol of the Friday sermon. The mosques in small villages were not permitted to have *minbars,* while in the larger cities, at first one Friday mosque, *masjid al-jumʿa,* and only later, several, were allowed to exist.

The form of the mosque which corresponded to all these requirements and was shaped by the development of them, was and remained simple: a large sanctuary, *ḥaram,* on the *qibla* side and a courtyard, *ṣaḥn,* to which the *ḥaram* opened. Arcades, *riwāqs,* may appear on three sides of the *ṣaḥn.* Mosques without a *ṣaḥn,* generally those smaller in size did exist from the earlier periods onward. The *miḥrāb,* the *minbar,* the minaret and the *maqṣūra* were the essential features of this simple enclosure.

The *Miḥrāb*

Although the origin of the *miḥrāb* is still being discussed, the word *miḥrāb,* in the Koran, refers to a temple (Koran, XIX : 12).[1] Because the *qibla* wall, *ṣadr,* is sufficient to indicate the direction of Mecca without the addition of a niche, some authorities have seen it not only as a place of specialized importance for the *imām,* but also as an imitation of the apse of the Christian church. In support of the latter Lammens points out that it was in general use only in the second century A.D..[2] For Stern the *miḥrāb* symbolically commemorates the customary place of the Prophet.[3] Al-Balādhurī says that the places where the Prophet used to perform his prayers in the Masjid al-Ḥaram and in the *masjid* at

---

[1] Over the Turkish *miḥrābs* part of this is written "then he came forth unto his people from the sanctuary (*miḥrāb*), etc...'

[2] Quoted by Diez, article 'Miḥrāb', in *EI*[1], vol. III, p. 485.

[3] H. Stern, "Les origines de l'architecture de la mosquée Omeyyade", *Syria,* vol. XXVIII (1951), p. 272.

Medina were held in great reverence.[1] As a niche for the *imām*, the *miḥrāb* achieved the practical effect of saving a rather large space otherwise unused and it probably did carry with it the symbolical meaning denoted by its Christian origin.

For the earliest mosques we have no evidence that a *miḥrāb* was used; the first Mosque of ʿAmr at Fustat (A.D. 642), one of the oldest in Islam outside Arabia, is known not to have had a *miḥrāb*.[2] It seems to have been introduced during the Umayyad period and its appearance generalized by the Early ʿAbbāsid period. Perhaps found, at first, only in the important Friday mosques, the *miḥrāb* was common to all mosques in the subsequent development of the Muslim architecture.

*Miḥrāb*s gradually assumed a large importance in the scheme of interior decoration. Umayyad *miḥrāb*s are known to have been richly decorated.[3] That special attention was given to the *miḥrāb*s may, in part, be due to the fact that they were associated with the *maqṣūra*s used by the caliphs or governors who also functioned as *imāms*. Thus the *miḥrāb*, was both a symbol of status and an architectural element for liturgical purposes.

In general there is only one main *miḥrāb* in a mosque; however there may be, although not very frequently, several *miḥrāb* niches on the *qibla* wall or other walls which face the same direction. In the Great Umayyad Mosque at Damascus, (706-714/15 A.D.), three *miḥrāb* niches were built.[4] There were also commemorative *miḥrāb*s which were attached to sanctuary columns facing the courtyard; to dedicate a *miḥrāb* to a great mosque and thereby to associate one's name with it seems to have been customary in Egypt. In the mosque of Ibn Ṭūlūn in Cairo there were *miḥrāb*s of the caliph al-Mustanṣir and Sultan Lājīn.[5]

The plan of a *miḥrāb* niche may be rectangular, polygonal or semi-circular. Even in the largest mosques it rarely exceeds a few meters in width and is usually covered by a decorative semi-cupola (a conch), betraying a post-Roman influence; the earliest examples are flanked by columnettes which carry an archivolt. The earliest dated *miḥrāb*, the Miḥrāb al-Khāṣṣakī, which came from a ninth century mosque, now in the Baghdad Museum, is a case in point. (Pl. I). Following the same lines is the oldest *in situ miḥrāb* in the mosque of Ṣidi ʿUqba at Qairawān, in Tunisia, dated A.D. 862/3.[6] (Pl. II).

*Miḥrāb*s, as the center of interest in the decoration of the mosque interiors offer illuminating examples of styles in the various regions and periods. A great variety of materials, such as terracotta, stone, wood, precious stones, stucco and faience, with elaborate carved and painted designs were used to decorate the *miḥrāb*s and the *qibla* walls around them. (Pl. III-VIII).

THE *Minbar*

Before the prayers, or after, it was customary for the Prophet to preach to the congregation. At first, when his followers formed only a small gathering he spoke while leaning

---

1 Balādhurī, quoted by PEDERSEN, *op. cit.*, p. 326.

2 Abu Hurairah, quoted by DIEZ, article '*Miḥrāb*', *EI*[1], p. 486. CRESWELL thinks that there was a *miḥrāb*, but that it was not concave. Cf. his *EMA* I, p. 28.

3 In the Mosque of Medina, built after A.D. 707, the *miḥrāb* had a revetment of marble and precious stones. CRESWELL, *EMA* I, p. 98f.

4 CRESWELL, *EMA* I, pp. 114 ff.; the fourth *miḥrāb* is a recent addition.

5 DIEZ, article '*Miḥrāb*', *EI*[1], p. 486.

6 The date is controversial: see CRESWELL, *EMA* II, p. 313f.

against one of the columns of the interior. But when the group grew large, he used a simple chair, *minbar* (from a stem meaning, 'to be high'), which had two steps and an additional one, *maqʿad*, for sitting.[1] According to Becker there is a possible connection between this simple *minbar* and the chairs of the *ḥakīms*, sages of old Arabia. [2]

After the lifetime of the Prophet, the *minbar*, which had been a simple preaching chair, assumed a special function: it served as the pulpit for the *khuṭba*, the Friday sermon. It is accepted that the *khuṭba* was instituted during the Umayyad period. While the chair seems to have acquired status as a kind of throne in memory of the Prophet. Notably, Abū Bakr when he was proclaimed caliph received the community's oath of allegiance while on the *minbar* of the Prophet. And perhaps similarly motivated, Muʿāwiya desired to have it brought to Damascus.[3] It was during his reign that Marwān Ibn al-Ḥakam added six more steps below the original three so that, as one reached the seventh step it corresponded to the first of the Prophet's *minbar*.[4] The development of the *minbar* as a significant architectural furnishing is a direct result, then, of its symbolical associations.

While to deliver the Friday sermon from the *minbar* is accepted as a *sunnah*, the position of the minbar became fixed only in later periods. Muhammad's chair stood, according to al-Bukhāri, near the middle of the *qibla* wall. Abu Mūsa is said to have placed his *minbar* in the center of his mosque at Basra, whereas Muʿāwiya used to transport his *minbar* with him.[5] It seems that the Umayyads used *minbars* equipped with wheels and that the *minbar* of the Great Mosque at Cordova had wheels.[6] However it eventually came to be placed to the right of the *miḥrāb*. The number of *minbars* also varied at first: Ibn al-Faqīh says that there were five in the mosque at Jerusalem and Maqrīzi says that four were ordered but not executed for the Madrasa of Sultan Ḥasan in Cairo.[7] In our day one *minbar* is usual.

Fittingly, *minbars* received much attention in the decoration of the interior. Made of wood in the early period, in later Islamic architecture, stone, especially marble *minbars* of great size were common. Most noticeably in Ottoman architecture, *minbars* often assumed proportions out of keeping with the dimensions of small and medium-sized mosques. The number of steps no longer uniform, the developed form of a *minbar* consists of a door opening to the stairway which leads to a platform covered by a baldachin with a conical or domical roof. Diez has suggested that the baldachin form may have been carried to Western Islam from India by the Turks.[8] The side panels of the stairway and the platform were decorated with traditional arabesque and geometrical patterns and

---

1 The number of steps is not clear. According to Ṭabarī "it was a chair consisting of three steps, on the third and last of which the Prophet used to sit.", quoted by Creswell, *EMA* I, p. 9f; al-Zurqānī (*Sharḥ al-Mawāhib*, Būlāq, VII, p. 135) says that it had three steps and a 'mustarah'; quoted by Kufrali, article 'Cuma', in *Islâm Ansiklopedisi*.

2 Quoted by Wensinck, article '*Khutba*', *EI*[1], vol. II, p. 981.

3 Ṭabarī, quoted by Pedersen, *op. cit.*, p. 339.

4 Kufrali, *op. cit.*, p. 228.

5 Pedersen, *op. cit.*, p. 340.

6 al-Maqqārī, quoted by Creswell, *EMA* II, p. 143; see also: F. H. Jimenez, "El almimbar movil del siglo X de la mezquita de Cordoba", *al-Andalus*, 24 (1959), pp. 381-399.

7 Quoted by Pedersen, *op. cit.*, p. 341.

8 Diez, article '*Minbar*', *EI*[1], p. 500.

the doorways with muqarnas friezes. From North Africa, Egypt and medieval Turkish Anatolia come some of the most exquisite examples of wooden *minbars*. (Pl. IX-XV).

The Minaret

During Muhammed's lifetime, the *adhān* was given from a rooftop or from an elevated platform. For some time afterwards, it is known also that customarily the call was made either from in front, or the roof of the *masjid*. From the period of the four rightful caliphs, there comes no evidence for the existence of minarets. In India, Iran and Anatolia, until the fourteenth and fifteenth centuries there existed mosques, especially those of lesser dimensions, without minarets. [1]

The first appearance of a tower-like structure used as a minaret occurred in Damascus where one of the towers set at the corners of the Roman temenos, wherein the Great Mosque was built, served this purpose. Utilized during Muʿāwiya's reign, evidently these towers were the prototypes of those which were commonly built after the reign of al-Walīd in the early eighth century. The governor of Egypt, Maslama, is known to have demanded permission from the caliph to build four *ṣaumaʿa* at the corners of the mosque of ʿAmr at Fustat.[2] It is relevant to note here that the word *ṣaumaʿa*, at this time, referred to the square church tower of Syria which became the model for the early Syrian minaret.

Two additional words used to denote minaret are *miʾdhana* and *manār*. The former refers only to its function, *adhān*, whereas the latter, which is more commonly used, refers also to a lighthouse, watchtower, boundary stone, etc.[3] Thus *manār* is appliable to any tower-like form or structure used to signal or to watch or to light the way. In Iran and Central Asia the mosque minarets were related formally to signal and watchtowers, and those towers connected with other buildings such as *madrasas* and *ribāṭs*, very likely, were multi-purpose. We also know that in Syria, Egypt and North Africa, small rooms in the minarets provided temporary retreat for pious men. [4]

In the various regions of the Islamic realm, the form of the minaret differed. Square towers are characteristic in Syria, Palestine, North Africa and Spain. (Pl. XVI). Cylindrical minarets with exterior ramps which, on a reduced scale, imitated ziggurats, were built with the early ʿAbbāsid mosques of Mesopotamia. (Pl. XVII). In the ninth century, Ṭūlūnid Egypt introduced its own style which combined the Syrian and Mesopotamian types; it was cylindrical in the upper stages with exterior stairs, and square at lower stage. (Pl. XVIII). In the later architectural styles of Iran, Irak, Central Asia and India the minarets were cylindrical probably following an older tower tradition. (Pl. XIX-XXII). As Diez has observed, the Persian word *mīl*, used to denote tower, minaret, also means signal post. Star-shaped minarets of the Ghaznevids and the famous Quṭb Minār at Delhi are rather isolated examples. Indian architects also built polygonal minarets. In Turkey early medieval minarets generally followed Persian models except in the

---

[1] Diez, article '*Manār*', *EI*[1], vol. III, p. 231.
[2] Maqrīzī, quoted by Creswell, *EMA* I, p. 38.
[3] Pedersen, *op. cit.*, p. 334.
[4] *Ibid.*, p. 335; Diez, article '*Manār*', *EI*[1], vol. III, p. 228.

South where the Syrian type was common. Later, in the Ottoman period, slim cylindrical and polygonal shafts with conical roofs became the exclusive form for Turkish minarets. And under the Ottoman rule, this type was carried to North Africa and to all Near Eastern countries. (Pl. XXIII).

All minarets were, at first, detached towers. Even when they were incorporated into the composition of the mosque plan, minarets continued their independent existence and had only a superficial formal relationship with the mosque. The minaret as an organic part of the mosque or *madrasa* design is the creation of later Islamic styles in the Mamlūk, Tīmūrid, Ottoman, Ṣafawid and Mughal periods.

A specific number or location for the minarets was not determined in the early period. At the Great Mosque of Damascus the minarets were merely replacements for the pre-Islamic towers. Usually the single large towers of early mosques were placed on the side opposite to the *qibla* wall, either attached as at Qairawān or independent as at Samarra. In Iran and Afghanistan the Ghaznavids or Saljūq minarets were independent towers although not necessarily placed opposite the *qibla* wall. Often found built against the portal of the *ṣaḥn*, the minarets may also be attached to the *qibla* wall. In the Egypt of the early Mamlūk period minarets generally were built on the north wall of the *ṣaḥn* over the main entrance or at each end of the north wall of the *ṣaḥn*. In later Mamlūk compositions they were placed near the *ṣaḥn* entrance whenever the usually irregular Cairo building site would allow for this. The Quṭb Minār at Delhi was the first grand-scale minaret in Indo-Muslim architecture. (Pl. XXIV). The subsequent development of Indo-Muslim architecture, however, reduced the size of minarets so that they appeared as decorative elements which were symmetrically disposed at the corners of the *ḥaram* or the *ṣaḥn*. Turkey, by contrast, in the Ottoman period prescribed the number of minarets permitted and incorporated them completely into the architectural composition. Only mosques built by sultans were allowed to have more than one minaret. As a rule sultan mosques had two, placed at the junction of the *ḥaram* and the *ṣaḥn*, whereas the minaret of other mosques was often placed to the right on the wall opposite the *qibla*, juxtaposed with the entrance arcade. Several of the imperial mosques do however possess more than two minarets. Generally speaking, the tower form of whatever derivation, which was borrowed for a new religious purpose, developed in Islamic architecture from an awkward addition to an harmonious architectural element.

Minarets offered yet another opportunity for the display of decorative possibilities. Although only one balcony is required and is usual for the minarets of Iran and Central Asia, the number was sometimes increased for aesthetic reasons in later Mamlūk, Ottoman and Indo-Muslim architectures. And muqarnas found a very appropriate place on the minaret balconies to enrich their expression and plasticity. Other types of decoration appeared in profusion especially on the brick towers of eastern Islam; bricks or smaller terracotta elements, with or without glaze, geometrical patterns and ornamental inscription bands enlivened the surface with texture, shadow or color. Mamlūk architecture created an even more complex visual array: greater plasticity was achieved by the use of columnettes, rows of niches, decorative windows in addition to the usual complement of surface patterns and muqarnas. Together they make of the minaret a highly picturesque form. (Pl. XXV).

The *Maqṣūra*

Not strictly related to Muslim ritual, the *maqṣūra* resulted from the mundane requirement of safeguarding the life of the *imām* who was, in the early centuries of Islam, the caliph himself or a governor. In this context, the passage in Ibn Khaldūn's *Muqaddimah* which relates that the first *maqṣūra* was constructed for Mu'āwiya or Marwān Ibn al-Ḥakam is generally accepted.[1] There is another tradition, however, according to which it first came to be built for the caliph 'Othmān inside the mosque of Medina.[2] We might find confirmation as to the purpose of the *maqṣūra* by pointing out that on many occasions in the early period the governor's palace, *dār al-imāra*, was erected next to the *qibla* wall and sometimes had direct access to the *miḥrāb* area, for instance at the mosque of Ibn Ṭūlūn at Fustat.[3]

Set off by wooden screens at first, the *maqṣūras* later were an important factor in mosque plans influencing the dimensions and roof system of the central axis. In connection with the mosque of Medina and other early Umayyad mosques, such as the Great Mosque at Damascus, J. Sauvaget has forwarded the view that the central nave functioned as a processional area.[4] We are probably entitled to view it as simply a large *maqṣūra* to contain the retinue of the caliph. A highly developed example of *maqṣūra*, that of the Great Mosque of Cordoba built for al-Ḥakam II, in A.D. 961-8, may be seen as a reminiscence of the earlier *maqṣūras* with wooden screens. (Pl. XXVI). The early use of a dome over the *miḥrāb* bays points its significance as the place assigned to the leader of the religious community, and became a standard feature of the mosque design.

Characteristic of Saljūq architecture in Iran, a domed chamber occupies the area in front of the *miḥrāb*. The well-known domed chamber of Niẓām al-Mulk in the Masjid-i Jum'a in Isfahan is a prayer hall expressly built for Malikshāh. No doubt correct in his observations, Sauvaget views it as a *maqṣūra*.[5]

In various regions and periods, the insertion of a separate enclosure for princely use can be shown. Although not expressly documented, there is little doubt that the open *iwāns* with their side rooms of the great *muṣallās* of Central Asia or Khorasan were the *maqṣūras* for local rulers. Rooms with similar functions in later periods, also were provided with separate entrances. The great imperial mosques of the Ottomans, for instance, have a sultan's lodge, *khünkār maḥfili*, usually to the left of the *qibla* wall and screened off from the prayer room with its own entrance.

The *maqṣūras* as protected enclosures seems to have served occasionally as the treasury of the mosques where relics of the Prophet could be preserved and venerated.[6]

In our day the *riwāq* which separates the *ḥaram* from the *ṣaḥn* is called *maqṣūra* in the Indian mosques, and "the probably modern partition that divides the place of prayer from the rest of the mosque" in Egyptian mosques is also called *maqṣūra*.[7]

---

[1] Ibn Khaldūn, *Muqaddimah*, Cairo, 1322, p. 212 f., quoted by Pedersen, *op. cit.* p. 336.

[2] Maqrīzī, quoted by E. Lane, *The manners and customs of the modern Egyptians*, Everyman, reprint, 1966, p. 594.

[3] Maqrīzī, quoted by Pedersen, *op. cit.*, p. 336.

[4] J. Sauvaget, *La mosquée omeyyade de Médine*, Paris, 1947.

[5] J. Sauvaget, "Observations sur quelques mosquées seldjoukides", *Annales de l'Institut d'Etudes Orientales*, Alger, Tome IV (1936) pp. 81-89.

[6] Diez, article '*Miḥrāb*', *EI*¹, vol. III, p. 488.

[7] E. Lane, *op. cit.*, p. 85 and p. 594.

Places for Ablution [1]

Ṭahāra, a pre-requisite for *ṣalāh* which may be achieved by the act of *wuḍū'*, came to be accommodated for within the mosque precincts; according to Ṭabarī, it was an innovation of the caliph 'Omar. Thus fountains, pools or similar installations evidently develop from this period onwards. Originally the water was collected in a pool, *birka*, situated in the center of the *ṣaḥn*. (Pl. XXVII). But the followers of Abu Ḥanīfah refused to do ablution with standing water maintaining that it was impure and instead used a fountain with running water, *Ḥanafīya*. The pool or fountain [2] in the center of the *ṣaḥn* may have been both for drinking and ablution purposes. A similar construction in the courtyard of the great mosque at Damascus was called a *ḳafaṣ al-mā'* by Ibn Jubayr. Later, places for ablution were located near the entrance of the *ṣaḥn* and were called *mi'ḍa'a* or *mavaḍi'u*. Generally it has not been customary for ablutions to take place within the sanctuary, but for decorative purposes, for refreshment or drinking a small basin, *ṣihrīj* or *siqāya*, with a waterjet, *fawwāra*, or a *shādırwān* very often was constructed in the mosque. (Pl. XXVIII). The place for the ablution fountains, instead, has usually been at the center of the *ṣaḥn*, or, where there is no courtyard, on the entrance side. In larger mosques like those of the later Turkish period they may be placed on the outer facade of the *ṣaḥn* or *ḥaram* walls (Pl. XXIX), in these mosques the *shādırwān*s found in the courtyards are for decorative as well as functional purposes.

Other Liturgical or Ceremonial Elements in the *Ḥaram*

The *ḥaram* gives shelter to various secondary elements which are more or less directly related to its main purpose. And although the space and constructions provided for these functions form a peripheral consideration in the design of the mosque, they are inseparable from its vitality. The word *zāwīya* has been in use as a general term for places permitted for specific purposes. It applies, for example, to the cells, *ḥujra*, in which ascetics resided for extended periods and to the enclosures for religious education, called also *madrasa*. Included also under this term were the screened enclosures for the female worshippers, generally placed on the side opposite to the *qibla* wall, which were also referred to as *maqṣūra*. Coming under the latter term moreover were the raised platforms with railings for the *mu'adhdhin* in larger mosques (this platform is also called *dikka*.) In Turkey all these separate enclosures are referred to as *maḥfil*. (Pl. XXX).

In the early centuries of Islam the *minbar* was used to deliver the sermon. But in addition there was constructed a pulpit chair, *kursī* (Pl. XXXI), which is a tall chair with arms, fitted with a Koran stand, *raḥla* (Pl. XXXII), from which readings from the Koran and later, even sermons were given. Except in the very early period when even the state treasury, *bait al-māl*, was deposited and guarded in the mosque,[3] usually the most expensive and important items deposited in a mosque are copies of the Koran (*muṣḥaf*s). Various other articles present are Koran stands, candelabres, candles, prayer beads and several chests which contain household objects for the cleaning of the mosque. In later periods separate rooms were included for storage and other services. As a final item

[1] For terminology see Pedersen, *op. cit.* pp. 344-346.
[2] Called 'Shādirvān' in Turkish.
[3] al-Kindī and Maqrīzī, quoted by Pedersen, *op. cit.*, p. 349.

woven straw or textile mats and rugs for covering the floors, often donated by the worshippers, may be mentioned.

Although rare, special objects of reverence are the relics of the Prophet, most particularly specimens of his hair which are preserved in chests and are visited by the faithful. [1]

The Illumination of Mosques

In the early days torches were employed, especially for the last *ṣalāh*. Oil lamps were introduced during the time of Muʿāwiya and candelabres, *tannūr*s in the Fāṭimid period.[2] The main sources of illumination in later periods were great chandeliers and lamps suspended from domes or vaults and large candelabres on either sides of the *miḥrāb*. In this context we may mention that on the night of religious festivals and two great feasts, *ʿĪd al-Aḍḥā* and *ʿĪd al-Fiṭr*, it has been the custom, since the early Middle Ages, to light oil lamps around the balconies of the minarets.[3] In Turkey there is also the custom to suspend, between the minarets of the great mosques, illuminated writings of a religious and moral character, *mahya*.

Other Functions and Buildings connected with the Mosque

For a long time, following the precedent given by the home of the Prophet, the mosque continued as the core of political as well as social life. The ceremony of *baiʿa*, the institution of *khuṭba* and the introduction of the *maqṣūra* were all of political nature. Another important activity associated with the mosque was religious instruction. A portion of the formal education of a young Muslim has always been acquired at the mosque. The space set apart for teaching within the mosque, *madrasa*, later was housed in a special building. Yet characteristic of all later Islamic architectural styles has been the close association of the *madrasa* with the mosque.

Functionally a multi-purpose building from the outset, the mosque has always been surrounded by various secondary structures. Around the courtyard and in houses adjacent to the mosque there were living quarters for the manservants, *mu'adhdhin*s and *imām*s employed at the mosque and for the students. For them and also for the visiting travellers and the poor, there were kitchens and bakeries. All of these diverse services and functions which were found within the first mosques prompted the creation of several distinct building types later. There were combined, occasionally, more functions than one within one building, but in the most advanced stage of this development, during the Ottoman period for instance, each building served only one function. As a result, great architectural complexes came into being which provided for the welfare of the community and encouraged social intercourse. [4]

Mosques of Particular Importance

Some mosques in Islamic history have had an especially sacred character. Pilgrimage is made to certain mosques such as those built over the burial places of saintly men,

---

[1] Fragments of the Prophet's mantle are also very important relics. See Pedersen, *op. cit.*, p. 342.
[2] Pedersen, *op. cit.* p. 343.
[3] Ibn Jubayr, quoted by Pedersen, *op. cit.*, p. 344.
[4] The Fātiḥ and Süleimānīye complexes in Istanbul, and the Sultan Beyazid at Edirne are the most characteristic examples.

foremost among which is the mosque of Medina built over the tomb of the Prophet himself and those over the tombs of ʿOmar and ʿAlī and the shrine-mosques of members of the family of the Prophet in Iran and Mesopotamia. Among the three most venerated mosques of Islam the most important is al-Masjid al-Ḥarām in Mecca. (Pl. XXXIV). Although it has no special architectural quality the sacred objects and relics such as the Kaʿba, the so-called *Maqām* of Ibrāhīm and Zamzam-well which it contains have necessitated the addition of annexes to serve the requirements of the annual pilgrimages.[1] The mosque in Medina is second in importance, while the third is al-Masjid al-Aqṣā in Jerusalem, first built during the caliphate of ʿOmar and in large part rebuilt in later periods. While mosques such as these have a special distinction, there developed in Islamic architecture no differentiation by type as in early Christian architecture with the martyrium churches.

The Founders of Mosques

Congregational mosques, where the obligatory Friday noon prayers were held (*al-masjid al-jumʿa* [2]) were erected by the caliphs or their governors and by the sultans and the vizirs. At first each city had only one such mosque often connected with the *dār al-imāra*. But in observance of the tradition which says that "Allah would build a house in Paradise for those who build a *masjid*.", wealthy Muslims endowed their cities with a mosque and provided for its upkeep and its functionaries by establishing a *waqf*.

---

1 For a description of the Kaʿba see: C. Snouck Hurgronje, *Mekka*, 2 vols., Leyden, 1931.

2 *Masjid-i jumʿa* in Persian and *ulu jāmiʿ* in Turkish.

II

THE DEVELOPMENT OF EARLY MOSQUE ARCHITECTURE

Before the Umayyads

According to one *ḥadīth* there was a *masjid* in a village near Medina built by earlier immigrants and Helpers (*anṣār*) of the Prophet before the Hijra.[1] And during the lifetime of Mohammed many *masjids* and *muṣallās* came into being. At that time al-Masjid al-Ḥarām built near the Kaʿba in Mecca, although simply a small building without a courtyard, was already highly venerated as the result of honoring ancestral custom. However out of all these early buildings of Muslim worship, Mohammed's house at Medina, alone, is regarded as the Muslim mosque from which has derived the Islamic mosque tradition. This probably is due to the fact that the form of the Prophet's *habitat* which was so intimately connected with his place for worship was accepted as an example (*sunna*) to be followed. Whatever structural, constructional or decorative differences might arise, the basic shape of the mosque, throughout early Islam, was that of a simple building with porticoed courtyard: all mosques consisted of a covered space with a roof supported by pillars or columns, *ẓulla*, and an open courtyard, *ṣaḥn*, usually surrounded by arcades, *riwāq*.

Frequently during the early Arab conquests, churches, synagogues, fire temples or apadanas were converted into mosques. The joint use of churches by Christians and Muslims occurred in many newly conquered cities.[2] But it is in those cities which the Arabs founded that Muslim mosque architecture grew

The first mosque, built in Basra in A.D. 635, was actually a *muṣallā*, an open area delimited by a line traced on the ground.[3] Ṭabarī says that the mosque at Kufa, built in A.D. 636, covered a square area, the dimensions of which were curiously determined by shooting arrows from a central point, and was set-off by ditches from the surrounding area with a roofed but wall-less shelter on the *qibla* side.[4] Of similar simplicity was the first mosque at Fustat built by ʿAmr Ibn al-ʿĀṣ in A.D. 641/2; an enclosed shelter with a low ceiling, the roof of which was supported by the trunks of palm trees.[5] Perhaps heeding the Prophet, who stated that "the most unnecessary activity that eats up the wealth of a believer is building", early administrators appear to have refrained from erecting rich mosques.

---

[1] Pedersen, *op. cit.*, p. 317. Lane says that it was "founded by Muhammad on his flight and before he entered al-Madina", *op. cit.*, p. 593.

[2] Creswell, *EMA* I, p. 25f; p. 128f.

[3] *Ibid.*, p. 15, footnote 2.

[4] *Ibid.*, p. 16f.

[5] Maqrīzī, quoted by Creswell, *EMA* I, p. 28f.

The Umayyads

When the Umayyads came to power and established the first dynasty of Islam, architecture assumed its customary function of expressing the worldly power of the society. Although no seventh century Umayyad mosque has survived, we gather from the descriptions of the re-building of the mosques at Basra, A.D. 665 and Kufa, A.D. 670, that the scheme remained the same. (Fig. 2). In both of them there were five aisles on the *qibla* side and two on each of the others with flat wooden roofs carried by columns of stone. While in plan no novelty existed, in their spatial proportions they exhibited close affinities to Sassanian royal halls because of their very high ceilings. According to

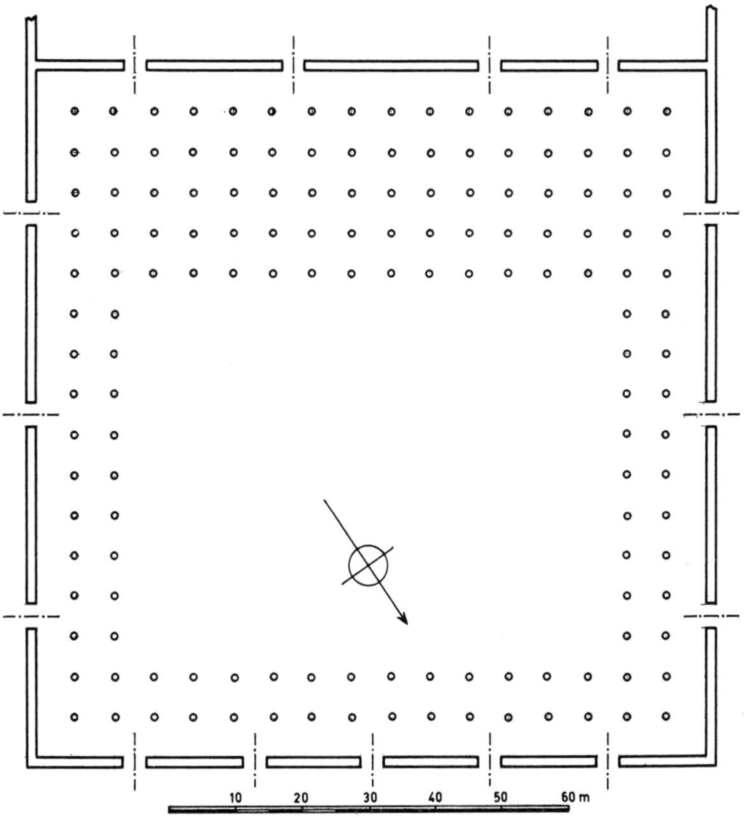

Fig. 2. Plan of the mosque at Kufa—Creswell's reconstruction.

Ibn Jubayr, the ceiling height in Kufa was thirteen meters.[1] In these mosques the *riwāq*s which surrounded the *ṣaḥn* became formal rather than functional elements. About their *minbar*s or *maqṣūra*s we have no knowledge. When the first mosque of ʿAmr at Fustat was rebuilt, in A.D. 673, a similar plan was adopted. It was the first mosque to have, by permission of Muʿāwiya, *ṣawāmiʿ* at the four corners.

From this period, the earliest existing mosque remains are those of the mosque at Wāsiṭ, the city built by al-Ḥajjāj between A.D. 701-4. Again following the scheme of

---

1 Creswell, *ibid.*, p. 36.

earlier examples, the only change in the plan is a single aisle around the *ṣaḥn* instead of two as at Basra and Kufa. [1]

During the reign of al-Walīd the Great Mosque at Damascus was built in A.D. 706-714/5, which is the oldest mosque still in use in its original shape.[2] One of the most discussed of the Umayyad mosques, it represents the early stage in the development of Islamic architecture. In it we find the first monumental expression of the Muslim ritual. Although the plan elements are more articulated and the directional emphasis is different, the mosque of al-Walīd is based on the traditional mosque scheme: a *ṣaḥn* surrounded by *riwāqs* which,

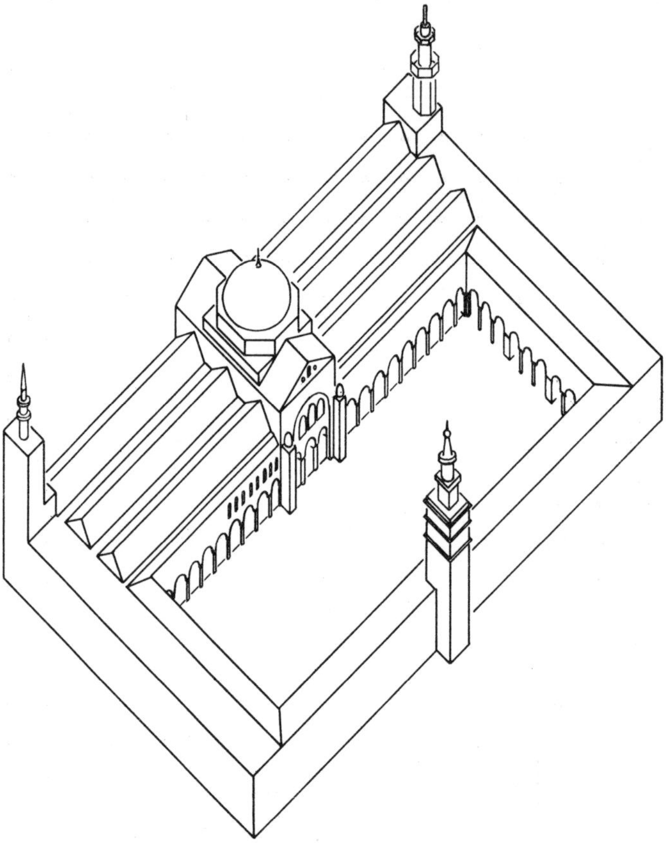

Fig. 3. Configuration of the Great Mosque at Damascus.

on the *qibla* side form three aisles, thereby composing the sanctuary, the *ḥaram*. (Fig. 3) (Pl. XXXV). Alterations brought about by the Syrian architects were the reduction of the number of aisles in the *ḥaram* and its division into two equal parts by the insertion of a central nave perpendicular to the *qibla* wall. The elongation of the proportions of the ground-plan from a square to a rectangle was due to the confirmation of the ancient temenos on which the mosque was built. Resting on double-tiered arcades, the roofs over the

[1] *Ibid.*, pp. 40-42.
[2] CRESWELL, *EMA* I, pp. 100-135.

ḥaram are gabled. The gabled roof over the central nave is higher than those of the aisles. Although subsequently rebuilt, the configuration of the present roof of the central nave comes from the time of the Saljūk sultan Malik shāh. Yet according to Muqaddasī, there existed a wooden dome over the central bay already in the tenth century and the entire *ḥaram* was then open to the *ṣaḥn*. Originally the mosque had three *miḥrāb* niches; the central one is accompanied by a *minbar*. The octagonal domed building on columns in the *ṣaḥn* is contemporary with the mosque, while Muqaddasī and Ibn Jubayr both call it the *bait al-māl*.[1] We are also told that the four corner towers of the temenos were retained for use as minarets. [2]

Of particular interest is the central axis of the mosque. Its form and function has been discussed by many scholars.[3] In plan and elevation it utilizes the traditional tripartite division and clerestory of some Syrian churches.[4] The facade of this central part may derive from those of Syrian churches and not, as has been suggested, from those of the palaces of the Late Roman architecture. In accordance with East Christian and especially Syrian ritual, the central nave of the church was assigned to clerical procession, whereas here the central nave probably functioned as a *maqṣūrah* for the caliph. The nave form was probably adopted by the Syrian builders because it was a familiar motif for a symmetrical facade.

In al-Walīd's mosque much expense and attention was given to the decoration, for it was to surpass all the churches of Syria in magnificence: the walls were covered with a marble revetment. The *miḥrāb*, now destroyed, was cut from a monolithic block of rock crystal. Iconographically, the most interesting part of the decoration is the mosaic revetment which covered almost all of the upper registers of the *ḥaram* and *ṣaḥn* walls.[5] The program of decoration, which does not include animate figures, was based on real and imaginary landscapes. Over the main *miḥrāb* there was a landscape with the Ka'ba to represent symbolically the direction of the holy city. On the *maqṣūra* walls, it appears that Medina was represented.[6] But representations of other famous cities, now greatly damaged by time and fires, which included Antioch and Constantinople, remind us of the strong secular undercurrent in Muslim religiosity.

The second great mosque of al-Walīd was that of Medina, from A.D. 707-9, which replaced the older Umayyad mosque built on the site of Mohammed's house. Descriptions of this mosque reveal similarities with the 'Irāqi type mosque, with the addition of four corner minarets and decoration of marble and mosaics. The first semi-circular *miḥrab* was introduced here by a Copt artist.[7]

In Jerusalem al-Walīd also rebuilt the *Aqṣa* mosque, although today very little remains

---

[1] *Ibid.*, p. 122, p. 141f.

[2] Although today only the lower register of the southeastern tower is pre-Islamic, its upper sections and the other minarets all date to subsequent periods.

[3] CRESWELL, *EMA I*, p. 112f; SAUVAGET, *La mosquée omeyyade de Médine*, pp. 122ff; O. GRABAR, "La grande mosquée de Damas et les origines architecturales de la mosquée", *Synthronon*, Bibliothèque des Cahiers Archéologiques, Paris, 1968, p. 113.

[4] Such as R'safa, Qalb Lozeh, etc., in north western Syria.

[5] M. VAN BERCHEM, "The Mosaics of the Dome of the Rock and of the Great Mosque at Damascus", *EMA* I, pp. 149-228.

[6] R. ETTINGHAUSEN, *Arab painting*, Geneva, 1962, p. 28, believes that this decoration had a royal significance.

[7] CRESWELL, *EMA* I, p. 97-99.

from his rebuilding. Among other important Umayyad mosques are the mosque of Aleppo, now destroyed, built by Sulaymān (A.D. 715-17) which imitated the great mosque of Damascus, and the mosque within the great fortified enclosure of Qaṣr al-Ḥair al-Sharqī, from A.D. 728, with a three-aisled sanctuary and *maqṣūra* with clerestory, which is also a smaller replica of al-Walīd's mosque.

The great mosque at Ḥarrān, probably built in A.D. 744-50, is a square enclosure. From its ruins it is impossible to reconstruct the original shape of the central nave, but it seems to have had a particular emphasis. The only existing minaret is a square tower attached to the north wall which is placed off axis. Ibn Jubayr says that in the *ṣaḥn* there were three domed structures on columns, one being the *bait al-māl.* [1]

The descriptions and existing remains of these earliest mosques lead to the conclusion that a consistent concept of mosque design already had been developed with its main elements by the beginning of the seventh century. It seems that the simplicity and the unchanging nature of Muslim ritual and the force of canonical tradition (*sunna*) quickly determined the basic shape of the mosque. Modified, needless to say, according to existing architectural traditions: thus in Irak late Sassanian, in Syria post-Roman features prevailed, each with its own distinctive structural methods and construction materials.

The use of the dome over the *maqṣūra*, which was to become so characteristic a feature of later Islamic mosque architecture, was borrowed from the Syrian wooden dome tradition. Symbolically, it was connected with the caliph's spiritual as well as political power.

The Early ʿAbbāsids

The first ʿAbbāsid mosque was built in the center of Baghdad, the newly-founded circular city of caliph al-Manṣūr in A.D. 862. Known only from al-Khaṭīb's description, the mosque was a sun-dried brick building, the roof of which was carried by wooden columns. Its plan seems to follow exactly the ʿIrāqi mosque tradition. Later on, a similar mosque was annexed to it by al-Muʿtaḍid Billāh (A.D. 893/4), by opening the *qibla* wall of the first one. The *miḥrāb*, the *minbar* and the *maqṣūra* were all transported to the new *qibla* wall.[2] On the Syrian border at Raqqa another early ʿAbbāsid mosque, built in A.D. 772, shows the Syrian influence by its three-aisled sanctuary.

But what may be regarded as the crowning examples of early Islamic mosque design of Mesopotamian origin, were two mosques executed during the reign of caliph al-Mutawakkil. One, the great mosque of Samarra, covers an immense rectangular area. (Fig. 4), the main prayer room contains twenty-five aisles, perpendicular to the *qibla* wall with the central aisle a little wider than the others. Surrounding the *ṣaḥn* are *riwāqs* of different depths; on the eastern and western sides there are four aisles and on the north only three. All enclosing walls, including that of the *qibla,* were pierced with sixteen doors, apparently because of the vastness of the mosque area. Large square piers of burnt brick, now totally destroyed, supported a wooden roof. The minaret of the mosque which still survives, called al-Manarāt al-Malwīya ("twisted minaret"), stands apart from the north wall and rises above a square socle with an outer helicoidal ramp. On the east, west and north the mosque was surrounded by courtyards, *ziyāda*s, and the whole complex thus obtained

---

[1] *Ibid.*, p. 406.
[2] Creswell, *EMA* II, p. 32.

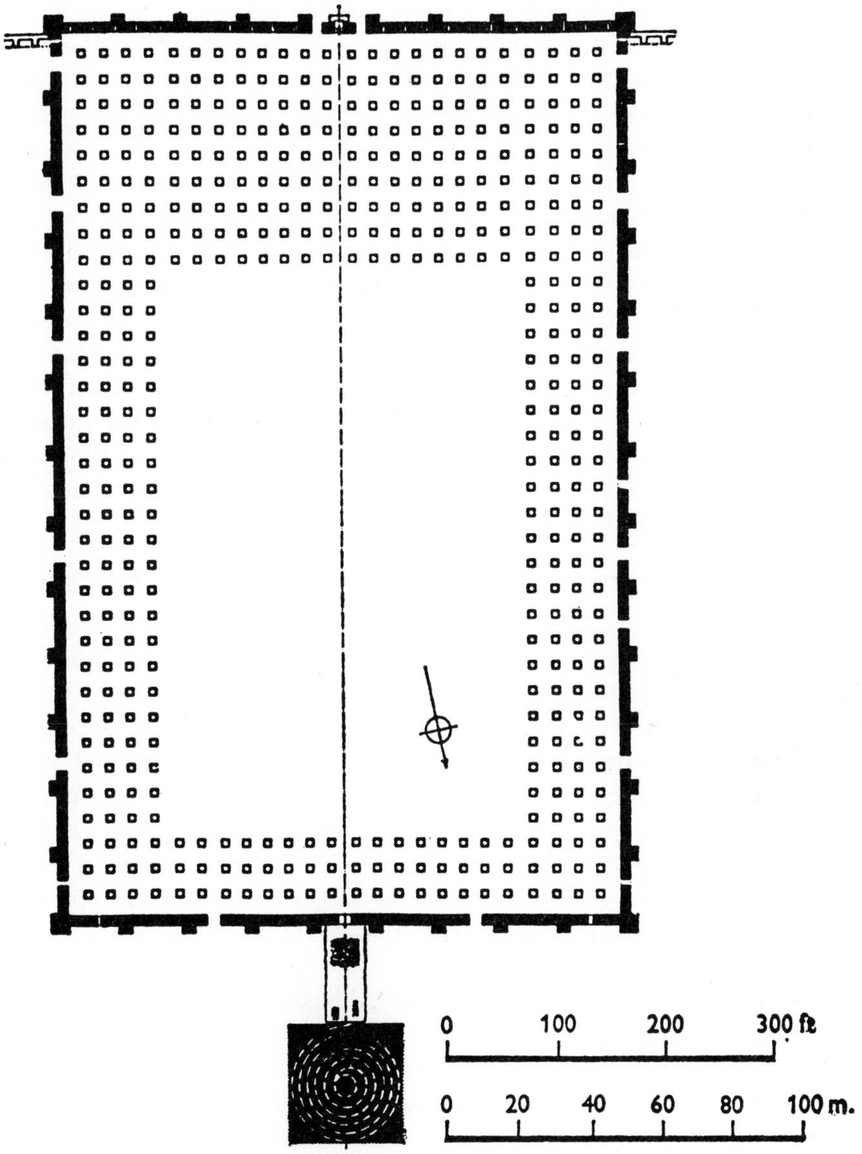

Fig. 4. Plan of the Great Mosque at Samarra—Creswell.

was again placed within a larger enclosure of great dimensions.[1] Of this mosque, the largest in Islamic history, remains to our day only a portion of the total height of the outer walls of the mosque proper. (Pl. XXXVI). Muqaddasī says that its mosaic decoration rivalled that of the great mosque of Damascus.[2] The *miḥrāb* was a rectangular niche —a characteristic of the early Mesopotamian mosques—defined by superposed arches supported by marble columns. That it was richly decorated is suggested by the fragments of gold mosaic on the spandrels. Its minaret, reminiscent of Mesopotamian ziggurats, is the earliest example of this type. However much colossal and awesome the mosque of al-Mutawakkil is in size, it nevertheless retains the primitive form of the earlier mosques of Irak.

Another large mosque, the mosque of Abu Dulaf, was erected by al-Mutawakkil in his private city, al-Ja'farīya, near Samarra. On the *qibla* side there are two aisles running parallel to the *qibla* wall, which might very possibly have served as a special area for the caliph and his retinue, in other words a *maqṣūra*. On the exterior a very large *mihrab* niche which projects from the *qibla* wall is a peculiar feature. Other arcades of the *ḥaram* which compose perpendicular aisles to the *qibla* wall are terminated at either end by T-shaped pillars, thus creating a more articulate space than that of the great mosque at Samarra where the detached piers must have produced a rather monotonous and directionless space. The minaret is a smaller reproduction of the Malwīya of Samarra. Here again there were open courtyards around the mosque which is in turn surrounded by long halls, i.e. *ziyādas*. (Fig. 5).

Architecture of the mosques in Egypt, North Africa and Spain during the Early 'Abbāsid Empire

Although they "varied widely in design" (Creswell) the mosques of this period were faithful to the essential concept of a mosque as a multi-support sanctuary combined with a courtyard and with a single minaret. Structural characteristics generally followed local traditions so that whereas in Irak mosques have detached supports, columns or piers, with rare exceptions such as the mosque of Abu Dulaf, in Syria, Egypt, North Africa and Spain they commonly have arcades, that is inter-connected supports, but both types have flat wooden roofs. The use of vaults for covering is not a characteristic of early mosque design, at least for the larger mosques.[3] Except in Egypt where the Ṭūlūnids imported the idea of exterior stairs of the Malwīya type, minaret design remained faithful to the Syrian square tower.

One of the important mosques of the 'Abbāsid period, although only partly preserved, is the Aqṣā Mosque at Jerusalem, rebuilt by the caliph al-Mahdī in A.D. 780. According to Creswell who proposed a reconstruction of al-Mahdī's mosque, it had a great rectangular *ḥaram* with fifteen aisles perpendicular to the *qibla* wall, the central one being much wider. In front of the *miḥrāb* and over the central bay there was a large wooden dome. There was no courtyard.[4] Possibly the Aqṣā Mosque of the 'Abbāsids was a mixture of 'Irāqi and Syrian traditions.

---

[1] 376 × 444 metres according to Herzfeld. See Creswell *EMA* II, p. 259.
[2] Creswell, *EMA* II, pp. 124-126.
[3] For early vaulted mosques see Creswell, *EMA* II, pp. 50-100 and 246-48.
[4] Creswell, *EMA* II, pp. 124-126.

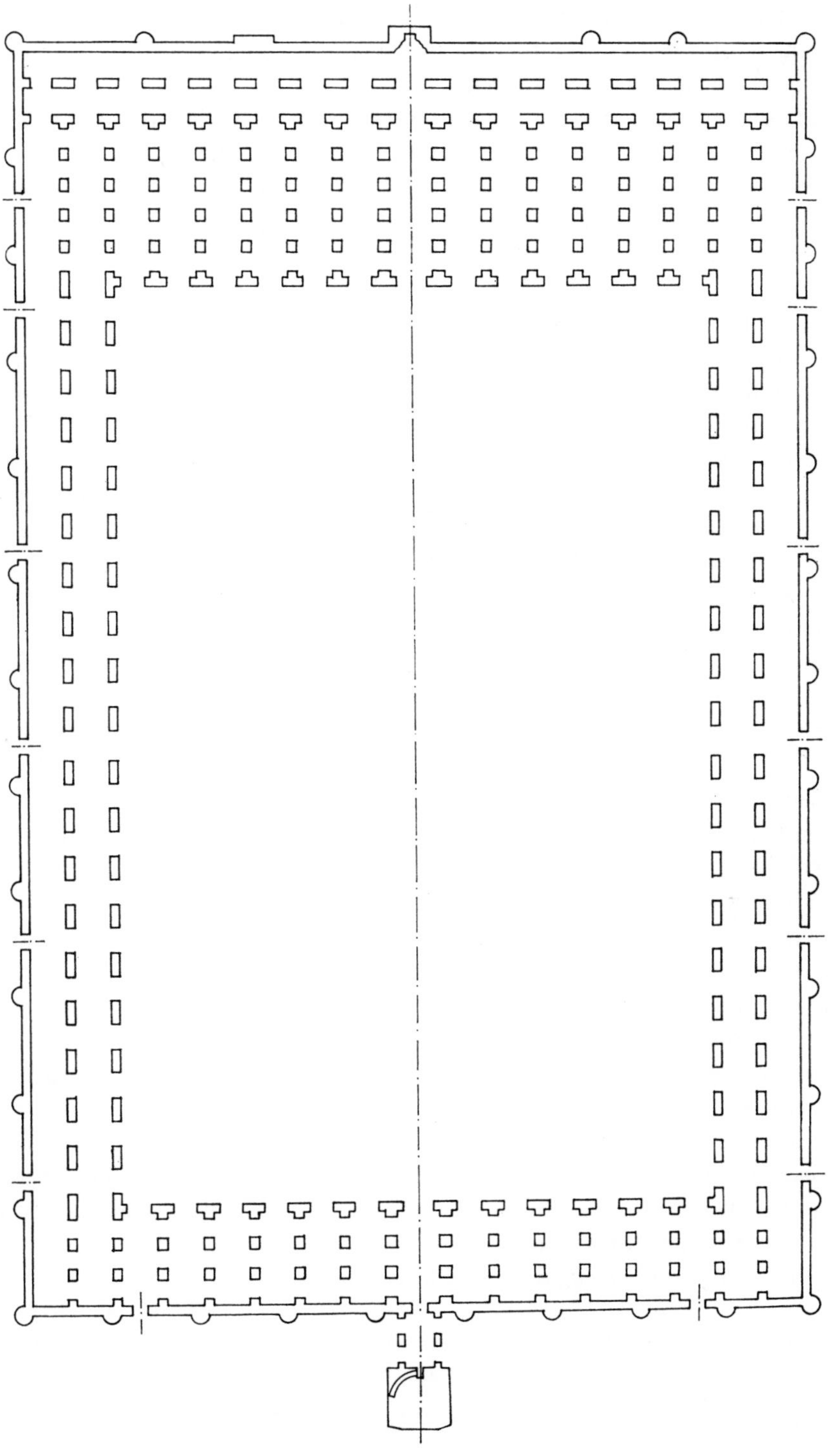

Fig. 5. Plan of the Mosque of Abu Dulaf at Samarra—CRESWELL

Three great mosques from Spain, North Africa and Egypt will suffice to represent the development of mosque architecture in the eight and ninth centuries; of these the Great Mosque at Cordova is the earliest.

The Great Mosque of Cordova, an elaboration of the Syrian design, was built first during the reign of ʿAbd-al-Raḥmān I in A.D. 785 and enlarged considerably afterwards by his successors. Again we find the early simple scheme of a courtyard and a hall covered with a wooden roof supported by arcades, of which the latter were the most characteristic aspect of ʿAbd-al-Raḥmān's building; apparently they were created by the necessity of re-using columns of insufficient height to which pilasters were added, after which both the columns and upper pilasters were linked by individual arches. (Pl. XXXVII). This system of double-tiered supports creates an impression of airiness and gives a more complex three-dimensionality to the interior space. This first mosque was, as suggested by Creswell, similar to the first Aqṣā mosque, with most of the architectural details also imported from Syria.[1] However the most conspicuous and attractive element at Cordova has continued to be the double-tiered arcade system, which has been retained with only minor changes in the successive enlargements. A very special feature of the mosque of Cordova, its rich *maqṣūra* which was built by al-Ḥakam II during the re-modelling begun in A.D. 961, is a rare example of a totally secluded room in front of the *miḥrāb* in western Islamic architecture. (Pl. XXVI).

The mosque of Sidi ʿUqba at Qairawān is the earliest extant example of North African mosques. It is a rebuilding by the Aghlabid ruler Ziyādat Allāh in A.D. 836, on the site of an earlier mosque built by the conqueror of North Africa, ʿUqba Ibn Nāfiʿ. Although some modifications were made at the end of the ninth century, it exhibits all the essential characteristics of early mosque design.[2] (Pl. XXXVIII). In the sanctuary seventeen aisles perpendicular to the *qibla* wall are covered by a wooden roof supported by arcades of marble columns. (Pl. XXXIX). The central aisle is wider and higher than the others; on either side are double arcade columns. Two domes, one before the *miḥrāb*, the other over the main entrance give more emphasis to the main axis. Another feature of the spatial arrangement is an aisle-like space parallel with the *qibla* wall which intersects with the central nave to form a T-shaped space core, a feature which is characteristic of many North African mosques. The minaret of the Qairawān mosque is the oldest existing in Islamic architecture (A.D. 836). A square tower of three storeys, the minaret, although connected with the north wall of the mosque enclosure, is structurally independent and has no organic dimensional relationship with the rest of the building. (Pl. XVI). Its well-preserved *miḥrāb*, probably also dated A.D. 862/3, which is the oldest *in situ miḥrāb*, is horseshoe in plan and in elevation, and is terminated by two decorative columns flanking the niche. It is decorated by the oldest known lustre tiles; the tiles were imported from Baghdad. (Pl. II). The *minbar*, again the oldest in Islam, is contemporary with the *miḥrāb*. (Pl. XI).

One of the best preserved specimens of early Islamic mosque building is the mosque Aḥmad Ibn Ṭūlūn in Fustat, built in A.D. 876/7-79. (Pl. XL). In structure and decoration it combines features of both earlier Umayyad and ʿAbbāsid architecture. (Pl. XLI).

---

1 *Ibid.*, p. 156f.
2 *Ibid.*, p. 212f.

The *ḥaram* is divided into five transverse aisles without any particular formal emphasis. The mosque is covered by a flat wooden roof and the area in front of the *miḥrāb* is accentuated by the usual small dome. The courtyard, in the center of which is a fountain, *fawwāra,* is surrounded by double aisles. Surrounding the mosque proper, except on the *qibla* side, are *ziyāda*s. (Pl. XLII). There was, on the *qibla* side, a *dār al-imāra,* in which, according to Maqrīzī, "the Sultan used to stop on his way to the Friday prayer. There he would repose, repeat his ablutions, and change his garments." The *dār al-imāra* opened to the mosque with a small door which led to the Sultan's lodge, the *maqṣūra,* near the *miḥrāb.*[1] Outside the mosque wall there were additional fountains for ablution, *mi'ḍa'a.* Within the northern *ziyāda* a four storey minaret was built; above the large square base of the first storey, there is a cylindrical second storey with an exterior staircase. The narrower, octagonal upper storeys are probably later additions. (Pl. XVIII). As in Samarra, the minaret is connected with the mosque by an elevated passageway.

Original with the Ibn Ṭūlūn mosque is its architecture of the façade. (Fig. 6). Appearing

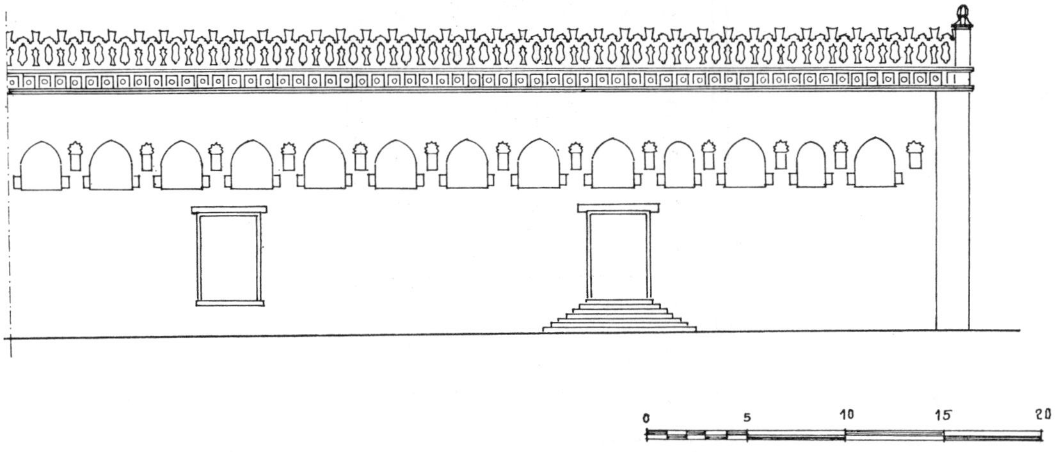

Fig. 6. Detail from the façade of the Mosque of Ibn Ṭūlūn in Cairo—Creswell

at the level above the door is a row of windows, between which are semi-circular niches. Both the windows and the niches have flanking columnettes supporting the archivolts. A frieze of simple framed squares pierced by small circular openings runs above the windows as a cornice and a decorative crenellation terminates the whole. As is clearly indicated by the decoration and by the shape of the minaret, Samarra greatly influenced the execution of the building. It is also quite possible that this façade is a faithful imitation of Mesopotamian examples.[2]

Mosque Architecture in Iran and Further East

No Iranian mosque of the first Islamic century has survived. As in Syria, existing buildings were converted into mosques in the early years of the conquest. From what is related by Muqaddasī, we can conjecture that the mosque at Iṣṭakhr (Persepolis) was,

[1] Maqrīzī, quoted by Creswell, *EMA* II, p. 000.
[2] Creswell, *EMA* II, p. 355.

in fact, a converted apadana which was probably in ruined condition.[1] We are told also that the Chahār Ṭāq of Yazd-i Khwāst was converted into a mosque.[2] Even the great *īwān* of the Ṭāq-i Kisrā at Madā'in (Ctesifon) served as a mosque. Nevertheless, the congregational mosques erected by the caliphs and governors, in the great centers of Iran were of the Arabian type.

The only Iranian mosque from the eight century which has come down to us is the Tārī Khāna at Damghan. (Fig. 7) (Pl. XLIII). It is a pillared hall with a courtyard, which is surrounded by a single aisle. But the system of construction, large pillars in burnt brick which support heavy vaults, creates a totally different interior, closer in spirit to the Sassanian halls than to the airy sanctuaries of Syria. It might have had a polychrome stucco decoration similar to that indicated by fragments found in other early Islamic

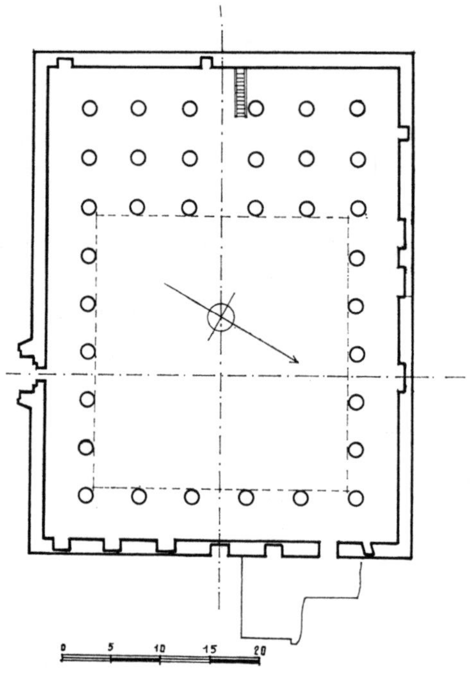

Fig. 7. Plan of Tārī Khāna at Damghan—GODARD.

building sites in Iran. The interior decoration of contemporary mosques rivalled the splendor of those in other ʿAbbāsid domains as exemplified by "the mosque at Nishapur which had marble columns, gold tiles and carved polychrome stucco." [3]

The very few remains from this early period is without doubt due both to modifications and rebuildings of later periods and to the ravages of time, which is particularly relentless in a land which builds in sun-dried brick. We know however that the original Arabic mosque plan was in use until the eleventh century and that the development of a specifically Iranian mosque type is the work of the Saljūq period. Other mosque types—the so-called

[1] *Ibid.*, p. 38.
[2] A. GODARD, *The art of Iran*, London, 1965, p. 261f.
[3] A. U. POPE, *Persian architecture*, New York, 1965, p. 81.

kiosque mosque, a domed square, and the *īwān* mosque, a barrel vaulted rectangular space open to one side which was sometimes joined by a domed square chamber—have not been found in their original forms.[1]

Other elements of cult, such as *miḥrābs*, *minbars* and minarets are not known from these early centuries.

General Remarks about Early Muslim Mosque Architecture

Although there exist mosques of different plan, especially mosques within palace complexes, such as the mosques in the palace of al-Walīd in Minya or that of the palace at Ukhaidir,[2] or the small Bū Fatātā mosque at Sūsa[3] and the ʿAbbāsid mosque at Balkh,[4] (Fig. 8) (Pl. XLIV), the basic mosque form established in the congregational mosques of the first cities founded by the Arabs in Irak and Egypt remained unchanged until the collapse of the first Islamic Empire in the tenth century, and persisted as a strong

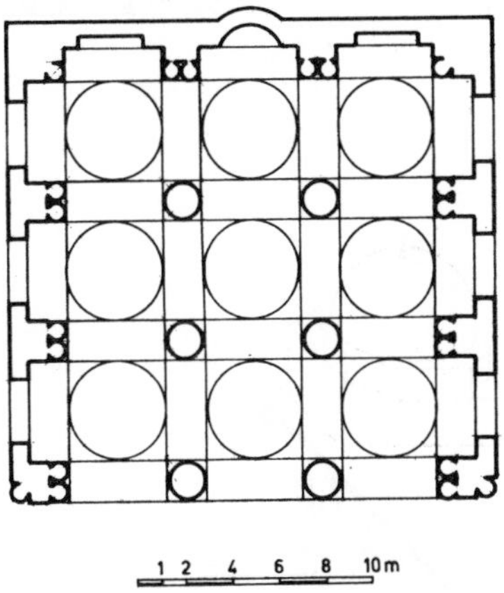

Fig. 8. Plan of the ʿAbbāsid Mosque at Balkh—Golombek's reconstruction.

undercurrent of the mosque design all over the Islamic realm. The basic scheme, however, was simple and flexible enough to be adapted to local architectural traditions which determined the character of regional developments of later Islamic styles.

In the organization of the mosque plan, the development of the central part of the sanctuary was a determining factor because of its connection with the *maqṣūra*. (Fig. 9a). Thus the function and form of the *maqṣūra* area which was shaped by the influence of local architectural traditions was the point of departure for regional differentiations. Local traditions were also the source, as we have seen in the foregoing pages, of the formal vocabulary of later developments. Yet the mosque itself, as a unique center for the social and cultural life of Muslim communities provided an atmosphere of creativity for specifically Islamic art forms. Even when executed with the use of forms created in former civilizations, the Arabic mosque was an original synthesis. And later, each muslim country in turn expressed its own synthesis in the architecture of their mosques.

---

[1] A. Godard, "Les anciennes mosquées de l'Iran", *Athār-e Īrān,* II (1936).
[2] Creswell, *EMA* II, pp. 74-76.
[3] *Ibid.*, pp. 246-48.
[4] L. Golombek, "Abbasid mosque at Balkh", *Oriental art,* vol. XV/3 (1969), pp. 1-17.

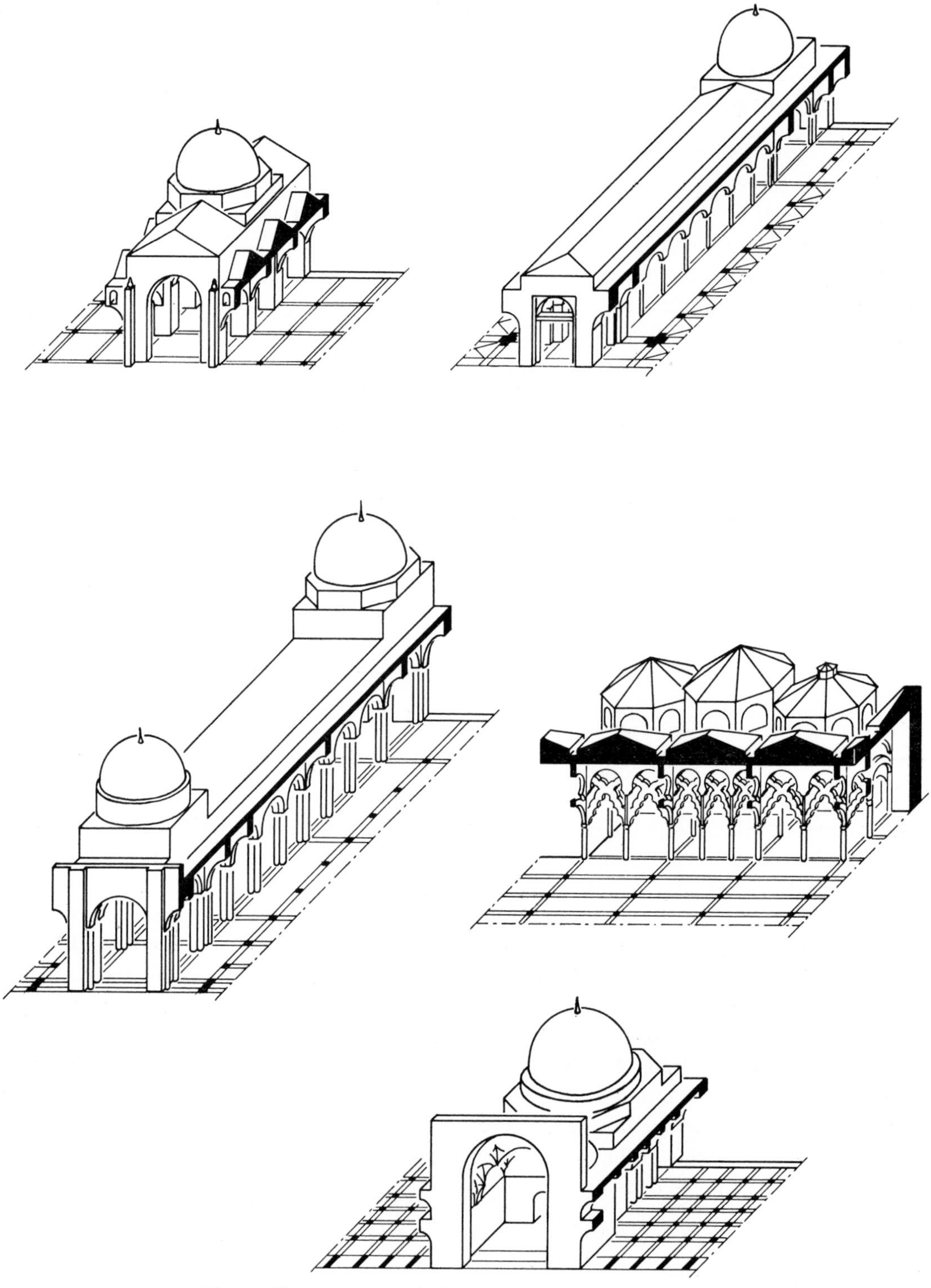

Fig. 9. The *maqṣūra* and the central part of the mosques

LEGENDS TO THE FIGURES IN THE TEXT

Fig. 1. The house of the prophet—Reconstruction according to CRESWELL's plan.
Fig. 2. Plan of the Mosque at Kufa—CRESSWELL's reconstruction.
Fig. 3. The configuration of the Great Mosque at Damascus.
Fig. 4. Plan of the Great Mosque at Samarra—CRESWELL.
Fig. 5. Plan of the Mosque of Abu Dulaf at Samarra—CRESWELL.
Fig. 6. Detail from the façade of the mosque of Ibn Ṭūlūn in Cairo—CRESWELL.
Fig. 7. Plan of the Tārī Khāna at Damghan—GODARD.
Fig. 8. Plan of the ʿAbbāsid mosque at Balkh—GOLOMBEK's reconstruction.
Fig. 9. The *maqṣūra* and the development of the central part of the mosques: a. Damascus-Great Mosque; b. Jerusalem—Aqṣā Mosque (CRESWELL's reconstruction); c. Qairawan—the Great Mosque; d. Cordova—the Great Mosque; e. Isfahan—Masjid-i Jumʿa

LEGENDS TO THE PLATES

Plate I

The miḥrāb al-Khāṣṣaki—Baghdad—(Late 8th or 9th century).

Found in the Jāmiʿ al-Khāṣṣaki in Baghdad and believed to be the *miḥrāb* of al-Manṣūr's mosque, this small niche (1.29 × 2.06 m) was carved from a marble monolith; now in Baghdad Museum.—Source: CRESWELL, *EMA* II, pl. 120d.

Plate II

The Miḥrāb of the Great Mosque—Qairawān—(862/3 A.D.).

During the rule of Abu Ibrāhīm Aḥmad of the Aghlabid dynasty the *miḥrāb* was decorated with marble panels and the surrounding wall with tiles imported from Baghdad, which are the earliest known luster tiles. The niche which has a horseshoe plan is 1.98 m wide and 1.58 m deep (CRESWELL) and flanked by marble columns. The semi-dome of the niche has a painted decoration.—Source: D. STEWART, *Early Islam*, Great Ages of Man Series, Nederland, 1968, p. 50f.

Plate III

The Miḥrāb of the Great Mosque—Cordova—(961-65 A.D.).

Built by al-Ḥakam II when he enlarged the mosque, the *miḥrāb* is a small room. Carved marble panels and mosaics are used for the decoration of the interior as well as the façade of the *miḥrāb* arch.—Source: F. C. GOITIA, *La Moschea di Cordova*, Forme e Colori, Sansoni ed., fig. 22.

Plate IV

The Miḥrāb of Uljaītū in the Masjid-i Jāmi'—Isfahan—(1310 A.D.).

The stucco *miḥrāb* was donated by the Īl-khān Uljaitu; it has rich, three dimensional floral decoration with *thuluth* and *kūfī* inscriptions. Single or double niches flanked by columnettes and placed in a rectangular frame are a common type of medieval Iranian *miḥrābs*.—Source: A. GODARD, *The art of Iran*, London, 1965, fig. 131.

Plate V

The Miḥrāb of the Madrasa Imāmī—Isfahan—(1354 A.D.).

A simple semi-circular niche decorated with mosaic tiles. Now in the Metropolitan Museum, New York—Courtesy, Metropolitan Museum, New York.

Plate VI

The Miḥrāb and Minbar in the Masjid-i Jāmi'—Yazd—(1375 A.D.).

A polygonal niche ending with stalactites; the whole surface is decorated with floral arabesques and calligraphy executed in faience mosaic.—Source: A. U. POPE, *Persian architecture*, New York, 1965, fig. VII.

Plate VII

The Miḥrāb of the Mosque of Ṭashkin Pasha in Damsaköy near Ürgüp—Central Anatolia— (Mid 14th Century).

A wooden *miḥrāb* now in the Ethnographical Museum of Ankara. Semi-circular niche enframed by friezes of *naskhī* script. Geometric and floral carving of delicate design—Source: Miss Yıldız Demiriz; Courtesy Ethnographical Museum, Ankara.

Plate VIII

The Miḥrāb and Minbar of the Madrasa of Sultan Barqūq—Cairo— (1384-86 A.D.).

Built by Sultan Barqūq, it belongs to the sanctuary (*līwān*) of the *madrasa*. The usual decoration of Mamlūk *miḥrābs* is polychrome marble panelling.—Source: M.S. BRIGGS, *Muhammadan architecture in Egypt and Palestine*. Oxford, 1924, Fig. 3.

Plate IX

The Miḥrāb of the Mosque of Rüstem Pasha—Istanbul— (c. 1561 A.D.).

Built for the Grandvizier Rüstem Pasha, a classical example of an Ottoman *miḥrāb* with tile revetment. The decoration consists of floral motifs, stalactites terminating the *miḥrāb* niche and large inscription panels also in faience tile; a polygonal plan is usual for Ottoman *miḥrābs*.—Source: Archive of the Chair of the History of Architecture, Istanbul Technical University.

Plate X

The Miḥrāb of the Adina (Friday) Mosque—Pandua, Bengal—(1364 A.D.)

Built for Sikandar Shāh in the former capital of Bengal, this stone *miḥrāb*, although using the familiar scheme of a niche in a rectangular frame, has an entirely local aspect of design and decoration.—P. BROWN, *Indian architecture (Islamic architecture)*, Bombay, 1968, Pl. XXV/2.

Plate XI

The Minbar of the Great Mosque—Qairawān—(862/3 A.D.).

Built for the emir Abū Ibrāhīm Aḥmad, this earliest extant wooden *minbar* of Muslim architecture has the simple form of a pulpit consisting of a stair and a platform. "It measures 3.93 m. in length and 3.31 m. in height." (CRESWELL). The decorative elements are carved panels with floral decoration.—Source: CRESWELL, *EMA* II, pl. 89a.

Plate XII

The Minbar of the Great Mosque—Algiers—(1096 A.D.).

This wooden *minbar* on wheels of the Great Mosque is from the Almoravid period and retains the simple shape of the panelled *minbar* of the Great Mosque of Qairawān.—Source: L. TORRES BALBAS, *Artes Almoravide y Almohade*, Madrid, 1955, Lam. 39.

Plate XIII

The Minbar of the ʿAlāʾeddīn Mosque—Konya, Turkey—(1155 A.D.).

According to its inscription carved by *ustādh* Mangubarti from Ahlat (eastern Turkey); it is the oldest wooden *minbar* of Anatolia, and already has the classical elements of Anatolian-Turkish *minbars*.—Source: KÜHNEL, ERNST, *Die Islamische Kunst*, Leipzig, 1929, fig. 439, p. 432.

Plate XIV

The Minbar of Selīmīye Mosque—Edirne, Turkey—(1574 A.D.).

Built for Sultan Selīm II, the marble *minbar* is of great dimensions (height: c. 24 meters, length: 13.40 m.). For the Ottoman *minbars* of the classical period, architectural form became more important than the decorative aspect.—Source: Archive of the Chair of the History of Architecture, Ist. Technical Univ.

Plate XV

The Minbar of the Pearl Mosque—Lahore—(1645 A.D.).

Moti Masjid, The Pearl Mosque, built for Shāh Jahān in the Lahore Fort. The *minbar* of the palace mosque has all the simplicity of the Prophet's *minbar*.—Source: M. WHEELLER, *Splendors of the East*, London, 1965, opp. p. 86).

Plate XVI

The minaret of the Great Mosque—Qairawān—(836 A.D.).

Built when the old ʿUqba mosque was reconstructed by the Aghlabid ruler Ziyādat Allāh, this oldest extant Muslim minaret, built in stone is a square tower of three stories. (height: 31.50 m.)—Source: G. MARÇAIS, *L'Architecture musulmane d'Occident*, Paris, 1954, p. 13.

Plate XVII

The minaret of the Great Mosque—Samarra—(between 848/9 and 852 A.D.).

The form of this burnt brick minaret is reminiscent of Mesopotamian ziggurats, the best known of which is the ziggurat of Khorsabad. The conical body with outer ramp is raised above a socle 33 meters square. It was probably terminated with a domical wooden baldachin. (original height: more than 50 meters)—Source: M. WHEELER, *op. cit.*, opp. p. 32.

Plate XVIII

Minaret of the mosque of Ibn Ṭūlūn—Cairo—(876/7-79 A.D.)

This minaret consisting of a square lower stage and cylindrical upper stages has exterior stairs. It remains unique in Egyptian architecture. Yet it may be regarded as the starting point of the originality of Egyptian minaret design.—Source: D. Brandenburg, *Islamische Baukunst in Aegypten*, Berlin, 1966, from the jacket.

Plate XIX

The minaret of the Masjid-i ʿĀlī—Isfahan—(11th or 12th century A.D.).

The brick tower (the existing part is about 50 meters) is named after a Ṣafāwid *masjid* which was built near it, probably replacing an older one. Independent minarets were customary in Saljūq architecture.—Source: W. Blund, *Iṣfahān, Pearl of Persia*, London, 1966, fig. 11.

Plate XX

The minaret of Jam—Afghanistan—(Second half of the 12th century).

Discovered in 1957, the Ghūrid minaret of Jam is one of the best examples of East Iranian tower building. Geometric designs and inscriptions are executed in various materials, glazed brick, terracotta mosaics and stucco. Actual height is about 60 meters.—Source: A. Maricq and G. Wiet, *Le Minaret de Djam*, Paris, 1959, planche I.

Plate XXI

The Minaret of the Mosque of Ḥasan—Rabat—A.D. 1196.

Square minarets which followed the example of the earliest Syrian towers were customary in North Africa and Spain. Decorative surface patterns based on the interplay of arches were also common.—Source: G. Marçais, *L'Architecture Musulmane d'Occident*, Paris, 1954, p. 247.

Plate XXII

The minaret of the Masjid-i Kalān—Bukhāra—(1127 A.D.).

This Central Asian minaret built by Qarakhānid ruler Arslan Shāh with his mosque (now destroyed) refers to the common origin of towerlike structures of the eastern Islamic realm. It has the usual brickwork in geometrical patterns.—Source: *Historical Monuments of Islam in the USSR*, Tashkent, fig. 4.

Plate XXIII

Qutb Minār—Delhi—(about 1200 A.D.).

The minaret of the mosque of Quwwat al-Islām, built by the Delhi Sultan Qutb al-Dīn, this tower is related to the East Iranian and Central Asian tower tradition, here executed by local builders, in stone. The use of alternating semi-circular and triangular pilasters is of the same origin. The top two storeys were added in the fourteenth century.—Source: E. B. Havell, *Indian Architecture*, London, 1927, Plate 11.

Plate XXIV

A minaret of the Mosque of Sultan Aḥmed—Istanbul—(1609-17 A.D.).

Turkish minarets in the Ottoman period have simple polygonal or square bases and, generally, cylindrical shafts with one or more balconies. They received their classical shape in the second half of the fifteenth century.—Source: Archive of the Chair of History of Architecture, Istanbul Technical University.

Plate XXV

The minarets of the Azhar Mosque—Cairo—(Fifteenth century).

Egypt is the only North African country where an original and strictly local design for minarets developed. The two minarets of the Fāṭimid mosque al-Azhar, seen in this drawing, are from the late Mamlūk period. The one seen above the doorway was built by Qā'itbāy after 1477 A.D.; the other with double ending by Sultan al-Ghaurī (A.D. 1501-16)—Source: Briggs, *Muhammadan Architecture,* Oxford, 1924, fig. 27.

Plate XXVI

The Maqṣūra of the Great Mosque—Cordova—(961-65 A.D.).

Built by al-Ḥakam II, the *maqṣūra* in front of the *miḥrāb* is three bays wide and one bay deep. All three bays have decorative domes the central one of which is one of the oldest ribbed domes in the history of architecture. The *maqṣūra* area also has a rich mosaic decoration.—Source: C. T. Rivoira, *Moslem architecture,* London, 1918, p. 359.

Plate XXVII

The Pool for Ablution in the Ibn Ṭūlūn Mosque—Cairo.

Source: D. Stewart, *Early Islam,* Great Ages of Man, Life/Time, Nederland, 1968, p. 45.

Plate XXVIII

The Shādirwān of the Aya Sofya—Istanbul—(1740 A.D.).

Built in the courtyard of the Aya Sofya for ablution by Maḥmūd I, this fountain retains the classical form of Ottoman *shādirwān*s. However the domed roof on columns is a characteristic of the eighteenth century.—Source: Archive of the Chair of the History of Architecture, Istanbul Technical University.

Plate XXIX

Ablution fountains in the Mosque of Sultan Aḥmed—Istanbul—(1609-17 A.D.).

In the larger Ottoman mosques the fountains for ablution were often placed at the sides of the *ḥaram* or the *ṣaḥn,* below the level of the prayer hall.—Source: G. Goodwin, *A history of Ottoman architecture,* London, 1971, fig. 331.

Plate XXX

The Müezzin Maḥfili (*Maqṣūra for the Mu'adhdhins, or Dikka*) *in the Aya Sofya*—Istanbul—(between 1574-95 A.D.).

The marble *maḥfil* is an independent gallery on columns. Its form was probably introduced during the Mamlūks and later adopted by the Ottomans.—Source: Archive of the Chair of the History of Architecture, Istanbul Technical University.

Plate XXXI

Kursī in the Ayasofya—Istanbul—(between 1574-95 A.D.).

Even in their most elaborate form Turkish Kursīs are simple chairs. In Egypt they might have incorporated Koran stands.—Source: Archive of the Chair of the History of Architecture, Istanbul Technical University.

Plate XXXII

A Raḥla (Folding Koran stand)—(1258 A.D.).

Built for Sultan Keykāvūs II, this wooden *raḥla* (size: 0.29 × 0.67 m), brought from Konya, has an exquisite floral carving. Now it is in the Islâm Eserleri Müzesi in Istanbul.—Source: Archive of the Chair of the History of Architecture, Istanbul Technical University; Courtesy, Islâm Eserleri Müzesi, Istanbul.

Plate XXXIII

A Mosque Lamp—From Syria—(Early fourteenth century).

In glass or ceramic, mosque lamps of delicate design were produced from the thirteenth to the fifteenth centuries in Mamlūk Egypt and Syria, and later, especially of ceramic, in Ottoman Turkey.—Source: E. Kühnel, *Islamische Kleinkunst,* Würzburg, 1963, fig. 184; Courtesy, Metropolitan Museum of Art. New York.

Plate XXXIV

The Kaʿba and the Masjid al-Ḥarām, General view.—Mecca.

The first *masjid* near the Kaʿba was built during the lifetime of the Prophet. The *masjid* as a complex of buildings, however, is a product of later periods, especially the Ottoman. The last important reparation of the Kaʿba took place in 1629, during the reign of Murād IV.—Source: H. Glück, E. Diez, *Die Kunst des Islam,* Berlin, 1925, p. 139; from M. d'Ohsson.

Plate XXXV

The Interior of the Great Mosque—Damascus—(A.D. 706).

This interior view of the Great Mosque, parallel to the direction of the *qibla* wall, closely resembles a basilical church, which has made many scholars believe it to be of Christian origin.—Source: D. et J. Sourdel, *La civilisation de l'Islam classique,* Paris, 1968, fig. 47.

Plate XXXVI

Aerial view of the Great Mosque—Samarra—(848-852 A.D.).

The first Mesopotamian mosques were large brick enclosures, the exterior of which appears similar to the older desert fortification. Although built in burnt brick, the interior of the Great Mosque is entirely destroyed.—Source: D. et J. Sourdel, *La civilisation de l'Islam classique,* fig. 3.

Plate XXXVII

The Interior of the Great Mosque—Cordova—(785/6-87 A.D.).

This view of the first part built by ʿAbd al-Raḥmān I shows the characteristic double-tiered arcades of the interior which were reproduced in later periods. The arches are alternately of brick and stone voussoirs.—Source: D. Stewart, *Early Islam,* p. 46.

Plate XXXVIII

General View of the Great Mosque—Qairawān—(836 A.D.).

The rebuilding of the Great Mosque at Qairawān marks, in the development of North African congregational mosque design, the logical and almost perfect conclusion: the central end with a dome at either end, an accentuated first aisle parallel to the *qibla* wall, and a centralized minaret on the north side.—Source: CRESWELL, *EMA* II, Plate 49.

Plate XXXIX

The Interior of the Great Mosque—Qairawān—(836 and 862 A.D.).

The wider central aisle emphasized by double arcades, which were reshaped at the time of the rebuilding of the *maqṣūra* dome (CRESWELL) is evidence of the importance of the *maqṣūra* in the development of the mosque design.—Source: MARÇAIS, *Architecture musulmane d'Occident*, Paris, 1954, p. 14.

Plate XL

The Mosque of Ibn Ṭūlūn, General View—Cairo—(876/7-79 A.D.).

Source: CRESWELL, *EMA* II, pl. 96.

Plate XLI

The Interior of the Mosque of Ibn Ṭūlūn—Cairo—(A.D. 876/7-79 A.D.).

The arcade system is formed by rectangular piers with corner colums which is of Mesopotamian origin. The strong directional emphasis produced by aisles running parallel to the *qibla* wall is stronger in the Ibn Ṭūlūn Mosque than in any other early mosque.—Source: CRESWELL, *EMA* II, Pl. 99.

Plate XLII

The Northeast Ziyāda of the Mosque of Ibn Ṭūlūn—Cairo.

The mosques were enlarged in later periods because of the increasing number of believers. But *ziyāda*s also appear to have served the crowds for Friday prayers or feast days, and are contemporary with the early mosques.—Source: BRANDENBURG, *Islamische Baukunst in Aegypten*, fig. 73.

Plate XLIII

Tārī Khāna—Damghan—(Second half of the 8th century).

The traditional large brick pillars and parabolic arches to support heavy vaults, creates in this early North Iranian mosque a specifically Iranian character.—Source: A. U. POPE, *Persian architecture*, New York, 1965, fig. 71 (top).

Plate XLIV

Remains of an 'Abbāsid Mosque—Balkh—(9th Century A.D. ?).

A simplified version of the pillared hall, the nine domed sanctuary seems to have a common origin not yet fully identified. In Central Asian secular building tradition, however, buildings consisting of a nine domed chamber exist. (PUGACHENKOVA).—Source: L. GOLOMBEK, "Abbasid Mosque at Balkh", *Oriental Art*, XV/3 (1969), fig. 4.

PLATES I-XLIV

The Miḥrāb al-Khāṣṣaki, Baghdad Museum.
(Source: Creswell, *EMA II*, Pl. 120)

Plate II

The *miḥrāb* of the Great Mosque, Qairawān.
(Source: *Early Islam*, Great Ages of Man, Time/Life p. 50; or EI^1 Art. Miḥrāb)

The *miḥrāb* of the Great Mosque, Cordova.
(Source: F. C. Goitia, *La Moschea di Cordova*, Forme e colori, Sansoni ed., fig. 22, in color)

The *miḥrāb* of Uljaitu, Masjid-i Jāmiᶜ, Isfahan.
(Source: A. GODARD, *The Art of Iran*, London, 1965, fig. 131)

Miḥrāb of the Madrasa Imāmī, Isfahan.
(Source: *The Metropolitan Museum of Art Bulletin,* Feb. 1965, Frontispiece)

The *miḥrāb* and *minbar*, Masjid-i Jāmiʿ, Yazd.
Source: A. U. Pope, *Persian Architecture*, New York 1965, fig. VII)

The *miḥrāb* of the Mosque of Ṭashkin Pasha, in the village of Damsa near Urgüp, Central Anatolia.
(Source: Miss Yıldız Demiriz)

Miḥrāb and *minbar*, Madrasa of Barqūq, Cairo.
(Source: M. S. Briggs, *Muhammadan architecture in Egypt and Palestine*, fig. 3)

The *mihrāb* of the mosque of Rüstem Pasha, Istanbul.
(Source: Archive of the Chair of History of Architecture, Faculty of Arch., Ist. Technical University)

The *mihrāb* of the Adina Mosque, Pandua, Bengal.
(P. Brown, *Indian Architecture* (*Islamic Period*), Bombay, 1968, Pl. XXV/2)

The *minbar* of the Great Mosque, Qairawān.
(Source: *EI*[1], art. Minbar)

The *minbar* of the Great Mosque in Algiers.
(Source: L. Torres Balbas, *Artes Almoravide y Almohade*, Madrid 1955, Lam. 39)

The *minbar* of the ʿAlāʾeddīn Mosque, Konya.
(Source: Ernst Kühnel, *Die Islamische Kunst*, Leipzig 1929, fig. 439, p. 432)

Minbar, Selīmīye Mosque, Edirne.
(Source: The Archive of the Chair of History of Arch., Technical University, Istanbul)

The *minbar* of the Pearl Mosque, Lahore.
(Source: M. WHEELER, *Splendors of the East*, London 1965, opp. p. 86)

Minaret of the Great Mosque, Qairawān.
(Source: G. Marçais, *l'Architecture musulmane d'Occident*, Paris, 1954 p. 13)

The *malwīya* of the Great Mosque, Samarra.
(Source: M. Weeler, *op. cit.*, opp. p. 32)

Minaret of the mosque of Ibn Ṭūlūn, Cairo.
(Source: D. Brandenburg, *Islamische Baukunst in Aegypten*, Berlin, 1966)

The minaret of the masjid-i ʿĀlī, Isfahan.
(Source: W. Blund, *Isfahan, pearl of Persia*, London, 1966, fig. 11)

Minaret of Jām, Afghanistan.
(Source: A. MARICQ, G. WIET, *Le minaret de Djam*, Paris, 1959, planche I)

Minaret of the Mosque of Ḥasan, Rabat
(Source: G. Marçais, *L'architecture musulmane d'occident*, Paris 1954)

The minaret of the Masjid-i Kalān, Bukhāra.
(Source: *Historical Monuments USSR*, fig. 4)

Quṭb Minār, Delhi.
(Source: E. B. Havell, *Indian Architecture*, London, 1927, plate 11)

The minarets of the mosque of Sultan Aḥmed, Istanbul.
(Source: Archive of the Chair of History of Arch., Technical Univ., Istanbul)

The minarets of the Azhar Mosque, Cairo.
(Source: BRIGGS, *Muhammadan architecture in Egypt and Palestine*)

The *maqṣūra* of the Great Mosque, Cordova.
(Source: C. T. RIVOIRA, *Moslem architecture*, London, 1918, p. 359)

Pool for ablution, Mosque of Ibn Ṭūlūn, Cairo.
(Source: *Early Islam*, Great Ages of Man, Life/Time, 1968, p. 45)

Plate XXVIII

The *shādirwān* of the Aya Sofya, Istanbul,
(Source: Archive of the Chair of Hist. of Arch.)

Ablution fountains in the mosque of Sultan Aḥmed,—Istanbul.
(Source: Archive of the Chair of History of Arch.)

Plate XXX

The 'müezzin mahfili' (*dikka*) of the mosque of Aya Sofya, Istanbul.
(Source: Archive of the Chair of History of Arch.)

The *kursī* in Aya Sofya, Istanbul.
(Source: Archive of the Chair of the History of Arch.)

Plate XXXII

A *vaḥla*, folding Koran stand.
(Source: Archive of the Chair of the History of Arch.)

Plate XXXIII

A mosque lamp, Goldmann Collection, Turkish, XVI cent.
(Source: Kühnel, *Islamische Kleinkunst*, Berlin, 1963, fig. 184)

The Kaʿba and the Masjid al-Ḥaram—general view.
(Source: H. GLÜCK, E. DIEZ, *Die Kunst des Islam*, Berlin 1925, p. 139, from d'Ohsson)

The interior of the Great Mosque, Damascus.
(Source: D. et J. SOURDEL, *La civilisation de l'Islam classique*, Paris, 1968, fig. 47)

Aerial view of the Great Mosque, Samarra.
(Source: D. et J. Sourdel, *Ibid.*, fig. 3)

The interior of the Great Mosque, Cordova.
(Source: *Early Islam*, Life/Time, p. 46)

General view of the Great Mosque, Qairawān.
(Source: *EI*[1], Art. Architecture. Pl. XVI)

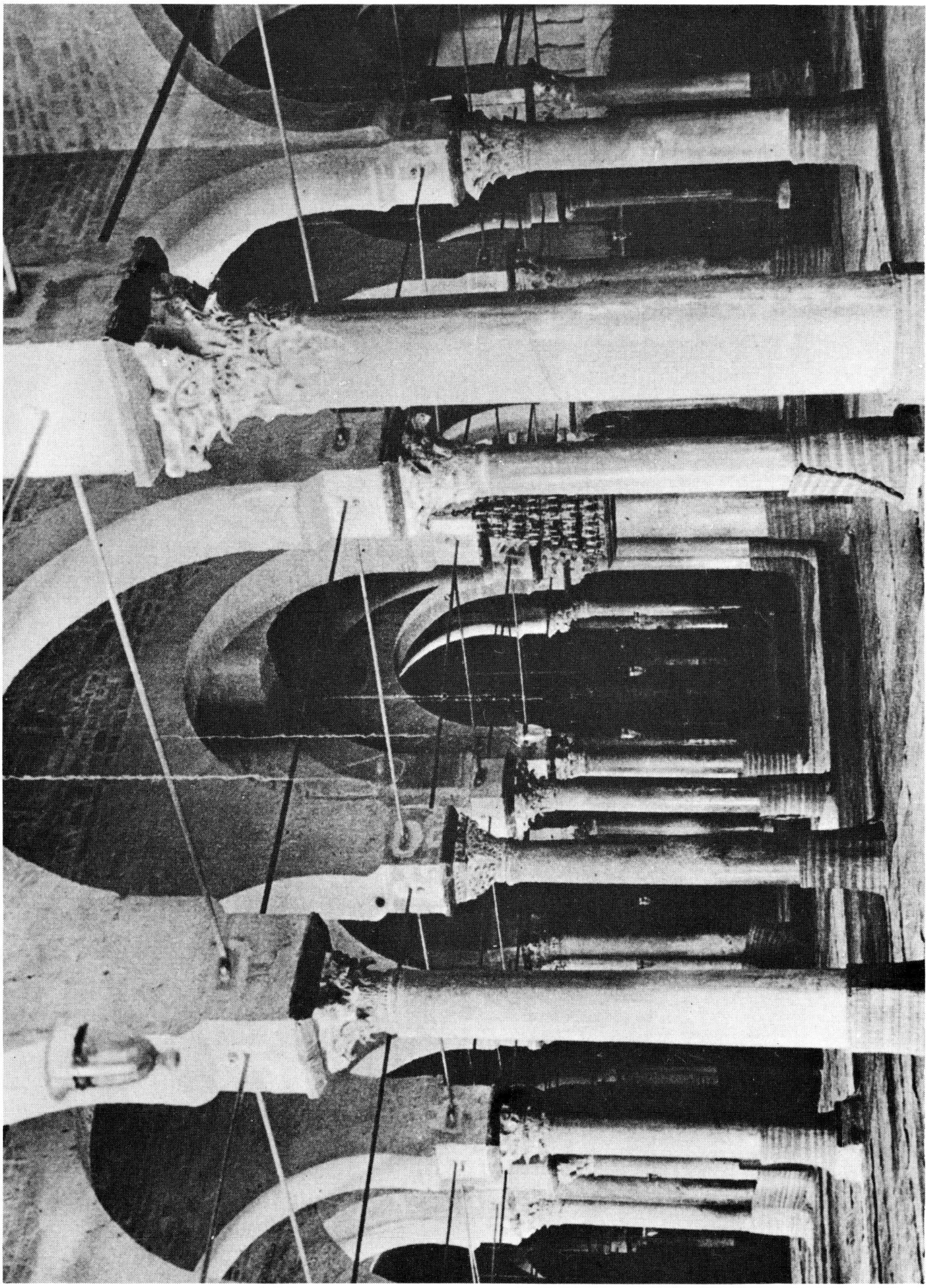

Interior of the Great Mosque, Qairawān.
(Source: MARÇAIS, *op. cit.*, p. 14)

Plate XL

General view of the mosque of Ibn Ṭūlūn, Cairo.
(Source: Creswell, *EMA* II, pl. 96)

The interior of the mosque of Ibn Ṭūlūn, Cairo.
(Source: Creswell, *EMA* II, pl. 99)

Plate XLII

Northeast *ziyāda* of the mosque of Ibn Ṭūlūn, Cairo.
(Source: BRANDENBURG, *op. cit.*, fig. 73)

Tārī-Khāna, Damghan.
(Source: A. U. Pope, *Persian architecture*, New York, 1965, fig. 71 (top))

Plate XLIV

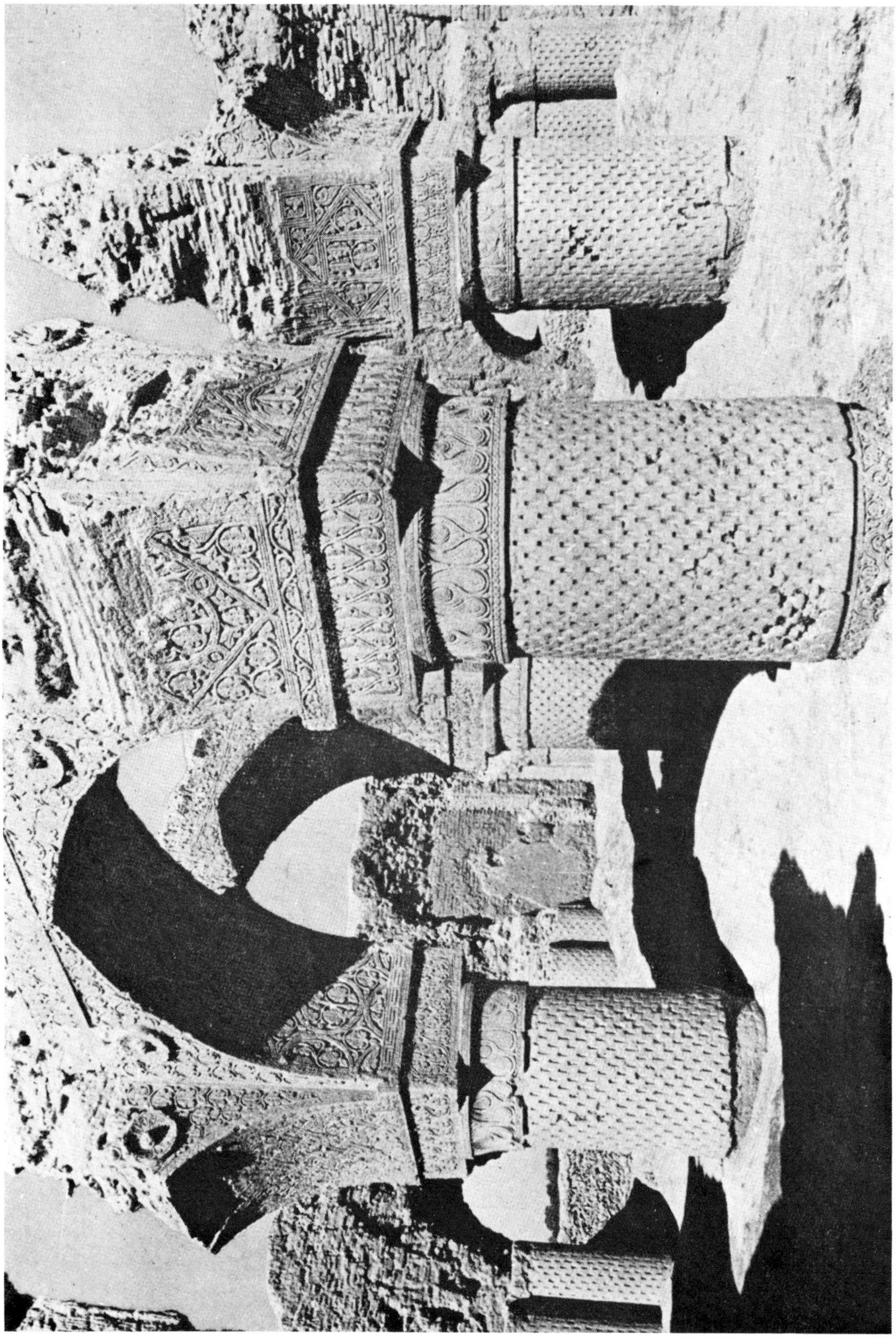

Remains of the ʿAbbāsid Mosque, Balkh.
(Source: L. Golombek, "Abbasid mosque at Balkh", *Oriental art*, XV/3 (1969), fig. 4)